THE GREAT DECEPTION

BIBLICAL ILLITERACY AND BLIND INDOCTRINATION IN THE DENOMINATIONAL CHURCH

by

GAIL TREBESCH OPPER

March 2012

Jenny & Bob,
     Thanks for
all you do in
Trailer Estates.
     Hope you
enjoy my Christian
journey. It changed
my life forever.
Hope the book is
a blessing to you.
          Gail Opper

THE GREAT DECEPTION

Biblical Illiteracy and Blind Indoctrination in the Denominational Church

By Gail Trebesch Opper

I dedicate this book to our children and grandchildren—April, Ryan, Adam, Bruce, Noel and Ethan. May your lives and the lives of many others be changed forever, as mine has been, by the words on the pages that follow.

To everyone who made this book possible, how can I ever thank you? Special thanks to my husband, Thurman, who pressed me to write the book and encouraged me every step of the way. To my brother, Bud, who remains an inspiration as an example of faith and love for God, even though he died when I was 13. To my sister, Lois, and posthumously to my brother-in-law, Dane, whose years of praying on my behalf led me to the Holy Spirit, who showed me another way. To Peter Alexeas, who told me many times over the years to write a book. To my cousin, Joe True, who painstakingly accepted the arduous task as original editor of the book. He did an incredible job of encouraging me as well as critiquing my work. To my final editor, Melanie Votaw, who forced me to work hard as well as humbled me and awakened me to changes that would make the book easier to read. To my Lutheran pastor, who eventually read the Bible from cover to cover and changed the lives of many, including me, through his new knowledge of Scripture. To the Holy Spirit, who instilled faith in me and gave me words for this book when I needed them. To Jesus, who died to save me. To God the Father, who gave me courage to write this book. Finally, to my parents, Earl and Alma Trebesch, who taught me to use that courage in God's service.

CONTENTS

INTRODUCTION

The world is nearing spiritual death, and America is second only to Europe in the digging of its grave—a grave dug by deception.

Unlike Europe, however, the root of this problem in America is not a lack of church attendance, though such attendance should be much better. Since the vast majority of Americans say they believe in God, the problem doesn't stem from a lack of belief. The problem isn't even that there are too few people who call themselves "Christians."

The impending spiritual death in America today, if not the world, is because people who say they believe in God don't have a clue who He really is. And those who call themselves "Christians" are unaware of the dangerous truth of that statement.

Americans are either spiritually dead or on the road to spiritual death because they are biblically illiterate. Every week they go to the same church they have attended for generations, often as heritage and tradition dictates, but they have little biblical basis for such attendance. If biblically challenged, they would be forced to admit their spiritual decay. Their faith is built on sand—sand laid down by churches who have, for centuries, written their own Bibles rather than studying the entire book God left for them to teach. When churches do study portions of the Word, it is with a bias of inherited doctrine rather than simply the guidance of the Holy Spirit, as God intended. Their conclusions are, therefore, skewed, and those conclusions are passed from generation to generation as if they were inerrant biblical truths.

Americans are steeped in tradition but oblivious to the fact that they've been led down a path to their own spiritual death. More importantly, churches and their parishioners have done this for generations, much to Satan's delight. The Bible says that Satan is the prince of this world, and churches and their members have handed the reigns over to him almost without a struggle.

The problem with denominational churches lies, at least in part, in the seminaries that produce the pastors and priests who are responsible for shepherding God's flock. Like the seminaries that produce them, these shepherds are often biblically illiterate and go on to instruct the flock, leading them to biblical illiteracy, too. As a result, both the clergy and the flock become nothing more than robots of seminaries and their hierarchies. Fully indoctrinated Christians using their robotic biblical illiteracy are responsible for unintentionally spewing half-truths and untruths everywhere they go. Church members do this because they believe what they don't bother to investigate, and they are loyal to a fault to those who have taught them. They are in denial, however, often due to this reliance on heritage and tradition. Without the necessary investigation, this cycle continues from generation to generation and has perpetuated for centuries. Blind indoctrination as a result of biblical illiteracy becomes the Christian norm.

At this point, you might be asking, "Can you prove your strong statements?" An experience from my years as a high school teacher offers one clarifying example. As an American literature teacher, I took my students briefly through the basic precepts of the Declaration of Independence and the United States Constitution so they could better understand the works authored by colonists, as well as the struggles those colonists endured so America could be free.

Once the students understood the basics, I gave them an assignment. They had 24 hours to find the words "separation of church and state" in the Constitution. To ensure they would all do the assignment, I told them that anyone who fulfilled it would receive an "A" for the entire semester—no tests, quizzes, or papers required. At the sound of the bell, students literally ran out of the room to find the answer they knew unequivocally was in the Constitution. Some spent every spare moment that day scouring the document (as a teacher I couldn't have been happier), while others simply searched for another teacher or a fellow student to hopefully give them the answer. Whatever method was used, they wholeheartedly believed they would find the answer easily in 24 hours, and an unearned "A" would be theirs.

Why were the students—semester after semester—so confident that they'd find such words in the Constitution? They had heard everywhere—even from adults they knew personally and trusted—that those words are indeed in the Constitution, so they felt they had no reason to question it.

Twenty-four hours later, however, the confidence from the day before turned to shock as they discovered that the words "separation of church and state" are actually *not* in the Constitution. What they found, in fact, was just the opposite. The Constitution actually says, "Congress shall not establish a national religion nor shall it prohibit the free exercise thereof." Nowhere does the Constitution suggest a "separation" or freedom *from* religion. Instead, it says there should be freedom *of* religion. My students (like many adults) had believed a lie; and, as I told them, the responsibility for the perpetuation of that lie rests forever with them and anyone else who believes *anything* without proper investigation.

The truth is not about what others tell us. It is what we research and learn to be true. Once we do the work and know the truth, we have been truly "educated." Before that, we are all simply robots of someone else's "truths."

Every week, parishioners in denominational churches throughout America and the world fall prey to this same kind of uncompromising belief in partial truths and untruths. You'll be amazed to discover in this book, and perhaps not willing to believe, that many churches do not share biblical truth in its entirety with their congregations simply because they don't know that truth. Parishioners, in turn, don't realize this because they haven't taken the time to discover the truth for themselves, even though this truth is available to all in Bibles that have been collecting dust in homes and churches everywhere. This cycle of "I'll believe it if you tell me" has gone on for thousands of years. People have relied on their churches, and pastors and priests have relied on their seminaries, to teach biblical truth. How do I know this? I've lived the life of an uneducated robot, too, just like my former students and perhaps you. That all changed for me, however, as I pray it will change for you. The only real truth is in the Bible, but how many people have actually read every word of it? Have you? I hope after reading this book that is exactly what you will do.

The Purpose of This Book

The pages of this book will carry you through the history of the "great deception" that churches have left with their parishioners. These churches have been deceived and have simply passed an incomplete "truth" on to you, like the belief that the "separation of church and state" is in the Constitution has been used to deny Christians in America their Constitutional rights. I believe many Christians, maybe even you, have been deceived, and I'm about to prove it.

My prayer is that this book will lead you to a hunger for biblical literacy and, thus, a need to read the Bible from cover to cover. If so, I must warn you that I won't make your biblical journey easy. Often, I won't tell you the source of a quoted passage from Scripture. The idea is to get you to read, study, and research the Bible on your own. That idea isn't unique with me. It actually came from God.

God said in His Word, "My people are destroyed for lack of knowledge" but "the truth shall set you free." According to Pastor Stan Pavkovich of Church of the Cross in Bradenton, Florida, "Everyone has rebellious kids—including God!" God's rebellious "kids" are perishing because they don't know the Word He left for them to read. They have refused to read it, believing it isn't necessary to do so. It is my prayer that by the end of this book, you will give up your rebelliousness, be set free, and rise from the spiritual death that plagues both America and the world—a death due to biblically illiteracy, blind indoctrination, and the craftiness of Satan.

PART I

"Study My Word"

CHAPTER 1

THROUGH THE EYES
OF A CHILD

It was 1949 and I was just four years old when I met Jesus at Gethsemane Lutheran Church in Warren, Michigan. The church building where we met is stark white on the outside and, even today, projects a beam that lights up the night sky 365 days a year. That beam was chosen by my mother as a guide in the night: "When you see that light come on, Gail, it's time to come into the house for the night." That light and its meaning guides my life to this very day, and I believe it was my first step to the brightest light I'll ever see one day when I close my eyes in death. The light was atop the church of my childhood. It illuminated an empty cross, lit at night to tell the world: "He is not here, He has risen, just as He said."

Gethsemane was only in my life for three short years, but it left an indelible impression on me. The lessons I learned in that small, unpretentious church cannot be measured. They are words that left Jesus' mark on my heart.

I loved going to church on Sunday. It was the one day of the week that I was expected to look my very best. Though I wore dresses to school, one or two were set aside for Sunday. I even had a hat, gloves, dress coat, and what my mother called "Sunday shoes." They were never worn to school. Mother explained to me that we look our very best for Jesus because He gave His very best for us. Every man, woman, and child in the church was "dressed for Jesus." Men were in suits; women were in hats, gloves, and heels. The children I saw wearing corduroy overalls and plain dresses every day in school were transformed once each week into angelic models from a fashion magazine. It was the first place in life where I learned to dress my best, and it wasn't a bad lesson to learn either.

Every Sunday morning a mini family reunion was held for me in that church. My dad's two sisters and one brother also attended the church, so it was a place for me to see my cousins every week, including one who was just six months younger than I. My older brother and my dad's youngest sister served as superintendents of the Sunday school. I was so proud to see them stand in front of the altar each week handling the opening service for the children. I can still sing the words of the songs I learned there: "Hear the Pennies Dropping" and "Sunday School is Over." Sunday school classes contained furniture just for children and were held in the small basement. Classes were separated by curtains hung with wire. The stories of Noah and the Ark, Moses and the parting of the Red Sea, King David, and, of course, the saving, protecting love of Jesus touched my heart weekly. I was a child who dearly loved the Jesus she met at Gethsemane.

Weekly church services followed Sunday school. Unlike today, there was no such thing as Children's Church. Children of all ages went to church with the adults. Whenever we sang, "There's a Church in the Valley by the Wildwood," I was certain that song was written about our church. I pictured the old country church I had seen in magazines, and I believed our church was a model for those.

The congregation was seated individually in brown, badly worn wooden seats that had undoubtedly been donated by a local movie theater. Each seat was separated from the next by a metal arm rest. The seats were a temptation for all conniving children who waited for the chance to pull the seat down from its back, sit down, and jump quickly off, to watch the seat bounce back into its once neatly folded position. Many times, the seat creaked. What fun to do that in the middle of the service, until we received "the look" from Mom or Dad, of course.

Everyone knew when the service was about to begin. The sound of a proud, well-practiced but small choir at the back of the church opened every service singing "The Lord is in His Holy Temple." This was the point at which either my mother or father, like clockwork, quickly gave me "the look." You know that look. It's the one that means, "Stop snickering; it isn't nice." Had that directive not been given, I would have proudly led a chorus of loud laughter among otherwise well-behaved children. You see, one lady was never on key but apparently believed she was because she was the loudest voice in the choir. Poor Mrs. Gottlieb, (names have been changed to protect people's anonymity), the organist and choir director whom I greatly admired, simply went on with the service, marching the choir up the aisle with one of the many hymns I had memorized over the years and still love to sing today. In fact, I could sing all four stanzas of most of the songs from memory. It's amazing how much those hymns have given me peace over the years. I should have known then that I loved music, but it would be many years later before I would discover that.

I can honestly say that I don't remember even one of the many sermons I heard in that church; but I still remember and appreciate the disciplines taught, such as sitting quietly for an hour, being respectful of others who were listening, and never talking. Despite what many people believe today, children are capable of listening well and sitting still for an hour. In my opinion, our time in church was good training.

That little white church didn't simply teach me about Jesus but showed me who He is through my observance of the way adults loved and served Him. Volunteers always gave their very best. In my mind's eye, I can still see Mrs. Schmiskey, a big woman, often with a cigarette in her mouth—ashes falling—in a tempered but flowered shirt dress with a middle belt, typical of the dresses of the day. She deep fried fish in the kitchen on Friday nights for the fish fries held during Lent, a six-week period of remembrance of the death of Jesus Christ. My favorite meal at Gethsemane, though, was the Mother/Daughter Banquets held each year in May. My own grandmother, though not a member of Gethsemane, always came and usually won the prize for the most children and grandchildren present. That made me proud. The small basement was filled to capacity every year for this special event.

Men were not exempt from volunteerism. A willing male hand was always available for needed repairs, and it remains remarkable to me that the church basement was dug by hand by the male members of the church. I wonder just how long it took them to do that.

Today it's difficult for me to imagine that my parents were only members of that church for a few years, and I personally attended there only from ages 3-6. The impact of Gethsemane on my life is remarkable and unmistakable considering our short time there. A family atmosphere existed in the church, and everyone cared about one another. Children were equally important. The adults cared about me, and I've never forgotten them.

Reaching a person for Christ definitely begins in childhood, and it begins with a church family that cares. Sunday school and Vacation Bible School are very important, even though few realize it until adulthood. My love for Jesus was firmly planted in my heart and soul in those early years at Gethsemane. Every time I hear the Bill Gaither Homecoming group sing "That Old Country Church," I realize the writer of that song had the same experience at his church as I had at Gethsemane.

Gethsemane Lutheran Church is an example for us all. It is important for us to recognize that churches will prosper only as children grow in the Lord and remain in the church. I have heard it said that America is one generation away from religious extinction, and I believe we're getting closer to that. Fortunately, though, God is always there and doesn't change. Religious extinction will not separate us from Him. He has assured us of that in the Bible. Realizing that America appears to be falling away from God, those in authority at churches everywhere must create a "Gethsemane" in the hearts of all children every day. I am so grateful to those who did that for me. Whenever I see a cross that is lit, I am reminded of the blessings I received as a very young child in that wonderful church. I ask you, then, is your church a "Gethsemane?"

Gethsemane Lutheran Church, 2009. It still looks much the same as it did in the 1950s, even with a cross on the steeple.

Christmas at Gethsemane Lutheran Church, 1943. Notice the children's chairs I so vividly remember as well as the curtain on the wire.

The bride enters the church at the side door, 1951. I, the flower girl, am directly behind her. Notice the basement wall dug and built by the men of the church.

Earl and Mary Louise (Griebe) Trebesch at Gethsemane's altar.

The bridal couple exits the church with my sister Lois behind them. Notice the chairs at the right with the flip-up seats.

CHAPTER 2

A GLIMPSE OF SALVATION

From the seed planted in my heart at Gethsemane, I remained in the Lutheran Church and became dedicated to it. I grew in my faith, as the Lutheran Church taught it, and shared that faith with others whether I was teaching Sunday school or Vacation Bible School or raising my own children. As the years went by, I became stronger in my beliefs, as the church taught them, and proudly stood up for them.

In 1953, my family moved to the Sunshine State. My parents were older and my dad hated the city job he had held for 25 years. He couldn't wait to retire, and he loved Florida when he and my mother visited there in 1949. Our five-day trip was, in itself, an adventure on two-lane roads up one side of a mountain and down the other side. Very few people moved anywhere back then, let alone moved out of state, and even fewer would leave their family and friends in a brand new Mercury pulling a 33-foot Pontiac Chief trailer behind them. It was the trip of a lifetime for me. My parents and I had more adventures than anyone could imagine. That is why we so enjoyed the movie "The Long, Long Trailer," which premiered that year starring Lucille Ball and Desi Arnaz. We had just experienced the very life that movie portrayed.

After we settled in a trailer park in Florida and I was enrolled in school, my parents began searching for a church. We weren't there long when they heard of a "drive-in" church in Venice. I was amazed at the fact that people could simply drive up to a speaker, remain in their car, and worship God. What an ingenious idea! It was so ingenious, in fact, that *Life* magazine's April 18, 1955, issue contained a story about the church. It was a two-story wood structure enclosed with glass. Pastor Robert White stood on the second floor within full view of the parishioners. On nice days, the floor-to-ceiling windows parted, and both the pastor and the choir could be clearly seen. Ushers would walk from car to car collecting the offering and serving communion to those unable to step out of their cars and go forward to the communion table at the base of the church. The first service at the church was held March 14, 1954, and there was room in the parking lot for 100 cars. Just imagine how much the reality of a drive-in church impressed an eight-year-old girl from Michigan.

The interesting thing is that the church was Presbyterian, and we were Lutheran. Back then, it was basically a requirement to stay in the same religion throughout your life. It was virtually unheard of to even visit a church that wasn't yours by birthright. My maternal grandmother actually sold a cottage on a beautiful Michigan lake because my mother was interested in a young Catholic boy there. People did things like that in those days. It was a sin in their eyes to desert the church of your people.

At that point in my life, though, I didn't think a thing about attending Venice Presbyterian Church rather than a Lutheran Church. I guess I was so enthralled with the idea of a drive-in church that nothing else was important to me. Years later, I would recognize what an eye-opening experience in my Christian life this church represented. It was, I believe, an initial step forward for me in my journey toward the Christ I came to know.

Venice Presbyterian Drive-In Church, Venice, Florida.

My dad boarded at a Lutheran high school in preparation for the ministry and moved on to a Lutheran college in the mid 1920s to continue his studies. Suddenly, he was attending a drive-in Presbyterian Church on a weekly basis. I realize today how amazing that is. It's clear that it was important to my parents to worship God somewhere, anywhere, and that worshipping Christ as our Savior meant more to them than the religion into which they had been born. That was a very unique thought at the time. This gift they gave me so many years ago—God first, religion second—would one day release me from the bonds of denominationalism.

My dad was unable to find steady work in Florida, and we were forced to move back to Michigan. That was one of the saddest days of my life. I absolutely loved Florida—the warm, sunny days; the white sand beach; the swaying palms; and the slower lifestyle. Though I would spend the next 50 years in Michigan, Florida was never out of my heart. I prayed that God would take me back there one day.

Michigan brought me back to my roots in relation to both family *and* religion. My parents moved to a small community northeast of Detroit and located a Lutheran Church there where we became members. I was confirmed in that church.

Confirmation is a church ritual where a child at about age 12 attends two years of instruction and then, publicly professes faith in Jesus Christ, receiving communion for the first time. Our confirmation classes met every Saturday for two years (though the pastor decided that I would only have to attend for one year).

I didn't know it at the time, but what we were actually learning was the doctrine of the church. I didn't know it because I didn't think about it. My parents told me I was going to the classes, and everyone in my family had done the same thing before me. It was just something I accepted. My classmates and I memorized the petitions of the Lord's Prayer, as well as the meaning of the Apostles Creed and the Ten Commandments, and we learned a great deal about Martin Luther and his disagreements with the Catholic Church. I enjoyed those classes and the pastor who led them.

Memorization was easy for me, and I loved to learn. Amazingly, though, it never occurred to me then or for the next 30 years that I don't believe we opened the Bible even once during those Saturday classes. In fact, I don't remember bringing my Bible with me when I went. Reading or memorizing the Bible was not required. *Luther's Small Catechism* was used during the entire class. Later, that realization would be a turning point for me. It became clear, as my eyes were opened, that what was most important in my church wasn't the Bible written by God for me to read, but it was the Bible according to Luther and its resulting doctrinal stand that mattered. In other words, the catechism classes were not a time of learning more about God and His Word but were simply my indoctrination into the beliefs of a denominational church. And indoctrinated I was!

My parents were a great influence on my Christian life, even though my dad died when I was 25. Having studied for the Lutheran ministry, he was extremely knowledgeable about the church and shared that knowledge with me. My mother had been a Sunday school teacher and clearly loved the Lord and her early years in the Lutheran Church. She guided me through my catechism memorizations and continued that guidance to adulthood for me. She used Bible verses to keep my brother, my sister and me in line: "God is everywhere and sees you when I don't." "Don't read your horoscope." Having two parents so devoted to their faith meant a lot to me then and means a lot to me today. We rarely missed church, and my parents, as well as other family members on both sides of our family who shared the same religion, kept me in the faith. It was a steadying influence in my life and one I still appreciate.

It was many years after I left home, married, and was busy raising a family before I began to wonder if, during my teenage years, my dad's eyes had been open to the reality of what I now call church indoctrination. Too bad his death prevented me from discovering the truth. Following church services every week when I was in high school, Dad would discuss the sermon at the dinner table (Lutherans are famous for their wonderful after-church dinners). He would talk about the things he agreed with and the things he didn't agree with. Most parents wouldn't have questioned a pastor or priest for fear their children might leave the religion of their heritage, but my dad was a very intelligent man who was relentless in his conversations. As a teenager, those sermon analyses seemed meaningless to me, but I always listened. The day came, of course, when they would become priceless. Somehow I'm sure Dad knew that.

One day, out of the blue, Dad stopped going to the very Lenten services he and Mom had attended for years and had taught me to attend. For those of you who don't know what I mean by Lenten services, six weeks before Easter, the Lutheran Church holds services on Wednesday evenings with the idea that we all need to search our hearts because of what Jesus' death on the cross did for us. It is, even to this day, supposed to be a time of serious introspection and reflection. As a youngster, I somehow got the notion that attendance at Lenten services was a requirement (and I really believe that both then and now, this is understood in the hearts of all good Lutherans: All good and Godly Lutherans go to Lenten services).

When Dad no longer went to those, I became very concerned about his salvation. I believed at that time that the rituals of the church—such as Lenten services— were both biblical and required. I had been taught that the pastor knew more than anyone else on earth about spiritual things because he went to the seminary. So, here was my dad not only questioning the pastor but also risking eternity. I never questioned Dad on this, but his lack of attendance at Lenten services seemed sacrilegious to me. Fortunately, any concern I had for my dad's salvation was put to rest the day I watched him die with incredible faith and courage. I know I will meet him in heaven one day, and I thank him for encouraging the faith I have today in Jesus Christ.

My dad's mother was perhaps the most Godly and faithful Christian woman I have ever known. My dad is one of eight children, and usually at our family gatherings, Grandma sermonized some of life's lessons for us as they appeared in the Bible. We then sang Christian songs. Grandma taught Sunday school for 50 years, taught Vacation Bible School, faithfully sent cards to shut-ins, and read her Bible from cover to cover. Following her and my grandpa's 50th wedding anniversary, she made a tape about her faith and her assurance of life after death, as well as her greatest hope that all of us would one day be in heaven with her. It is one of my special treasures. The Godly influence of her and my grandpa in my life simply can't be measured. I think I'd be a Christian today just so I wouldn't disappoint them and would someday meet them in heaven, as I now know I will.

Grandma's greatest impact on my life, however, came at the end of her days when she herself was a shut-in. Her Lutheran pastor would come to her home to serve her communion, and she discussed the Bible with him during each of his visits. Despite the fact that he was the seminary graduate who supposedly knew it all, he became aware that my grandma's knowledge of the Bible was so much greater than his that he stopped coming to visit her, saying that others needed him more than she did. That had to be difficult for my grandmother, but she got a pastor to think to the point that he was uncomfortable. If that caused him to search the Bible and question his faith, he has my grandma to thank for it ... and she gave me that same gift.

As I'm sure is true in most denominational religions, Lutheran pastors are, in their opinion and in the opinion of most members of their congregations, the only ones with the true spiritual answers. They learned in seminary just how important they are. They are the leaders of their flock and are responsible for keeping that flock Lutheran. They took an oath to remain true to Lutheranism. So, being challenged by one who didn't even complete high school—let alone a woman—would not have set well with a young Lutheran pastor in the 1960s. Grandma would never have allowed that to deter her, though. She had read the Bible from cover to cover and, at the end of her life, she saw God's teachings in His Word as far more important than the teachings of her pastor. How blessed I am to have been able to call her "Grandma."

Between my parents, grandparents and Godly relatives, I had a foundation that withstood many storms. I pray my husband and I have passed along that same foundation to our children, and I pray even more that they teach and live that foundation as an example to their children. Do the words we speak to our young children and the example we set make a difference? There is no doubt in my mind that they do. I carry the fruits of the labors of those who cared deeply about me and my spiritual life. Their faith was cemented in a denomination, as mine would be for many years. Though such devotion was the norm then and still is today, God has recently been opening the eyes of those who seek Him aside from their denominational heritage. Much to my surprise, I became one of them.

CHAPTER 3

INDOCTRINATION AND LOYALTY

In 1963, I graduated from high school and began my freshman year at Capital University, a Lutheran college in Bexley, Ohio, a suburb of Columbus. My dad had been a student there nearly 40 years before me and really wanted me to attend there. Though I had set my sights on a Michigan college and never really wanted to go to "Cap," as it was fondly called, I honored my dad and spent my freshman and sophomore years there. During my brief time at Cap, I would meet a lifelong best friend, many other great girls, and young men who were studying for the Lutheran ministry.

It amazes me to realize that in my weekly required religion classes, we never, to my recollection, used the Bible. I didn't think a thing about it at the time. I liked the religion professors and never doubted that they had read the Bible from cover to cover so I was sure that whatever they taught me had to be from God's book.

Not once during those college years did I ever question the core teaching of Lutheranism. Yet during the time I spent in church and at Cap, I became grounded in its doctrine. I was then—and really always had been—a proud and solid Lutheran but became even more so in those two years at Capital. Looking back on those days, I often think of the men I came to know pretty well who would eventually become Lutheran pastors. I never questioned what Capital's seminary was or was not teaching its seminarians. I trusted that the professors would teach the Bible in truth and purity and in its entirety. Of course, I should have been more aware and should have asked many more questions. Denominational blindness and indoctrination obviously had a stronghold on me, and it would be years before I'd recognize it.

I always believed that it was my dad who chose Capital for me, but I have come to understand that it was God who did the choosing. God knew that what I learned there would later lead me to a strong, knowledgeable, and personal relationship with Jesus Christ. This relationship would undoubtedly have been less profound had I not attended Capital and used my comradeship with the seminarians as well as my research into the seminaries of other denominational churches as a stepping stone to the truth. I met future pastors at Capital, watched some of their lives unfold, and gained the knowledge necessary to write this book. Nearly 40 years would pass before I would use what God had taught me there, but I know I would probably not have seen it had it not been for the time I spent at Capital. Isn't it amazing how God can use a time and place in our young lives to later change us forever to do His will?

In 1974, I married a man who, like me, had been raised Lutheran. We met at a Lutheran singles group—a meeting that was the dream of all good Lutheran parents. I have learned that denominational parents, not just Lutherans, desperately want their children to marry within the denomination of their heritage. Loyalty to a church and its traditions is passed down from generation to generation, and my husband and I were molded into that pattern and obediently followed it to a tee. We married and raised our three children in the Lutheran church, even sending our two oldest children to a nearby Lutheran high school. We never missed church, baptized and confirmed all three of our children, faithfully sent them to Sunday school and Vacation Bible School, and attended Adult Bible classes ourselves. In fact, we attended the same Lutheran Church for the first 17 years of our marriage. My husband was a trustee, while I taught Sunday school, Vacation Bible School, sang in the choir, and served at those wonderful church dinners Lutherans are known for. Neither of us could have ever imagined that this very church would one day be the place that would change our lives for the better forever for Jesus Christ.

I well remember the Sunday Adult Bible classes where one woman challenged just about everything the teacher presented. I thought, "Why doesn't she just leave if she's not happy? What gives her the right to disrupt our class?" The day she decided to leave the church for good, I was glad. Little did I know that in a few years, I would follow right behind her and begin to appreciate what she had said. That was, I'm sure, exactly what she hoped would happen. Many years later, I apologized to her for my blindness.

It wasn't long after the woman left our church before two amazing things happened almost simultaneously in the Christian lives of my husband and me. My husband began to have a heart for both aborted children and those who soon might be. A movement took root on a major thoroughfare in a Detroit suburb where Christians gathered one afternoon a year and carried signs denouncing abortion. My husband's eagerness to join those fellow Christians bothered me, and I balked at it for quite a while. After all, I had been raised in a society that believed you never spoke about religion or politics. I had been taught in church that God would handle the problem. All we had to do was trust Him. So the idea that I would stand along a busy highway carrying a political-religious sign embarrassed me. My husband really believed in the cause, though, so I decided to join him. To my surprise, I felt good that I was doing exactly what I felt God would want me to do—be His hands, feet and mouth for the unborn. I was shocked at just how good I felt about that experience.

While my husband got more and more involved in and devoted to the woes of the unborn, God had a plan for my life, too. One day, out of the blue, I inwardly began to cringe at the idea of attending weekly Lenten services. It dawned on me that Jesus' death occurred more than 2,000 years ago. Yet, every year, we Lutherans nailed Him to the cross again—for six long weeks. Jesus had actually been alive—resurrected—for more than 2,000 years, but we spent only one day of the year focused on that. I realized that Jesus was only on the cross for three hours; but as Christians, we had actually kept Him on that cross for nearly 2,000 years! At Lenten services, we walked around like mourners one night a week for six weeks and for what reason? He's alive; He lives; He's resurrected; He isn't dead. What a revelation!

Like my dad had done many years before, I stopped going to Lenten services. That really bothered my husband. Though I still honor Good Friday today and the sacrifice Jesus gave on the cross that day for me, I also recognize that I was—from that time forward—going to serve a *risen* Savior. Jesus' death on that cross did not by itself save us; people die every day. Though He went to the cross and carried my sins there, had He not risen from the dead, He would simply be a man who was born, performed miracles, witnessed, and was crucified. What made Him different is the fact that He rose from the dead and ascended into heaven. Though I'm definitely saved by the blood He shed on that cross, I'm freed by the resurrection. Jesus is alive, and I will live, also. Like so many others, however, I had spent a lifetime mourning Jesus' death yearly and had spent very little time celebrating His resurrection and life. Jesus died so that my sins would be atoned for, but He lives so that I, like Him, might also live eternally. I believe that years before me, my dad came to this realization and either purposely or unintentionally laid a foundation for me to follow his example without guilt. I was suddenly free from the ritualistic bondage I had felt during six weeks of mourning, but I now had a husband who didn't see things the same way. As a result, the situation with my husband became more and more complicated.

It wasn't long after my determination that I no longer had to worship Jesus' death for six weeks a year that our pastor preached the message that began the dramatic and unforgettable change in me. I would move forward from that one message and never look back. I don't recall his sermon topic that day or most of what he said. What I do recall are these life-changing words: "If you died today, do you know beyond a shadow of a doubt that you're saved?" I sat stunned in the pew. Somehow, it seemed that he was speaking directly to me. Sadly, I had to honestly answer "no" to that question, and I instantly knew there was something very wrong with my spiritual life. Jesus died and rose again that I might be saved. I knew that. God promised salvation to those who believed in His Son Jesus Christ, but I had doubts about my own salvation. If death came at that moment, I wasn't certain I'd go to heaven.

What in the world had I missed? I was raised in church by Godly parents with Godly grandparents as an incredible unit of support. I attended a Christian college. I raised my own children in the church. I had been baptized and confirmed. I taught Sunday school and Vacation Bible School. I read daily devotions with my children. Despite it all, I lacked the unquestionable assurance of my own salvation and never knew that until I heard the words spoken that morning by our pastor. How in the world was that possible? Even more puzzling was the fact that until that moment, I had no idea that I had no idea. The Holy Spirit was definitely tugging at my heart that day.

When church ended, I walked to the back—an area called the Narthex—and leaned against a podium with much concern. I knew I was in emotional trouble. Where would I go from here? That thought was daunting. For no particular reason, I glanced down at the podium's table where a pamphlet caught my eye. I had never seen anything like it before and have not seen one since. It was called "Bible Pathway," distributed by a ministry in Murfreesboro, Tennessee. It promised to lead me through a reading of the entire Bible in one year (the amazing thing about finding this pamphlet is the fact that only material published by Concordia Publishing House of the Lutheran Church Missouri Synod was allowed to be distributed in church. I will always believe God meant that pamphlet just for me, and He used someone to leave it where I would find it).

My heart pounded, and I was suddenly weighed down and burdened with the reality that I had never before read the entire Bible. I instantly understood that I was biblically illiterate. This had never occurred to me. It simply hadn't been that important. In that moment, I heard a "still, small voice" say to me, "How do you know that what your pastor has preached for a lifetime is biblical? He may be presenting heresy, but you wouldn't know it because you haven't investigated." That was so very true. I had spent more than 40 years in the Lutheran Church trusting pastors without question. This was despite the fact that I had attended a Lutheran college, knew Lutheran seminarians personally, and somehow deep inside now knew they, like me, hadn't read the Bible from cover to cover either. My denominational heritage was crumbling before my very eyes and not one notion about tradition or heritage was going to change that.

In reality, how can any of us refuse to read the *one* book in its entirety that God personally left for us—a book containing the words that God Himself breathed? For a lifetime, I had simply hidden behind a church and its seminary. I believed the pastors knew more than I could possibly know because they had surely read the entire Bible in seminary. I also got the impression the Bible was too hard for a non-seminarian like me to understand. In my heart, though, I now knew that wasn't true. In that moment of awakening, I said to myself: "Why would God write a book all about Himself and His purposes and make that one and only book too difficult for me to read and understand?" I had simply *believed* rather than *researched* (remember the separation of church and state story?) and made excuses for not having read the Bible myself. It was clear that it was time to change that.

Excuses for not reading the only book God left us would no longer work for me. This particular Sunday, God gave me a second chance. He told me that I had to read *His* book. He let me know that my salvation concerns were based on the fact that I had not personally read *His* Word. Suddenly, God was becoming more real. Instead of a God who, as I had always thought, was up there basically doing nothing but waiting for me to come to heaven one day, watching from a distance as I plodded along this path we call life, He became someone who really cared about me. He obviously wanted something more from me than I had been giving. He wasn't just sitting around waiting for me.

He was calling me that Sunday to get to know Him personally and let Him be my pilot through life. I was about to really meet God for the first time. No longer would I plod through life alone. Little did I know that from that day forward, God would lead, and I would follow—learning slowly to trust and obey. My whole life was about to change for the better.

Without hesitation, I grabbed the "Bible Pathway" pamphlet and left church with a new determination that one year from that very day, I would complete the reading of the entire Bible. It was the dawning of a new day for me—and a new life. Through the voice of one pastor, God had placed a personal, long distance call to me. It was now up to me to answer that call.

CHAPTER 4

THE JOURNEY BEGINS

I made a commitment to God that I would complete the reading of the Bible in one year and would allow nothing to interfere with that promise. I asked the Holy Spirit to guide me through every word and teach me as only He could. I prayed that the doctrine of my church, taught and reinforced in me for years, would not stand in the way of the things God wanted me to see in His book. Even then, I still believed that the church of my life had all the right answers. I was certain the Bible would only back up everything the church had taught me. Why would I ever doubt that? The Lutheran Church had stood the test of time for my ancestors, my grandparents, and my own parents. Members of my family were good, honorable people who I believed loved and served the Lord.

Only today can I look back and see the enormity of the miracle that took place that day at the podium in the back of my church. Had someone—particularly an elder or teacher—seen that "Bible Pathway" pamphlet before I picked it up, it would have been destroyed. How did it get there, and why was it there at just the right moment? Many would simply call it a "coincidence," but I don't believe in those. That was the day God began to take my faith from my head to my heart—where it had to be if I was going to be saved. Tradition, heritage, church attendance, being a good person, or even being a Lutheran taught under the auspices of Concordia Publishing House, was not going to save me. In fact, I believe today that being a Lutheran actually prevented me from seeing the truth.

God bless the person who either left the pamphlet on that podium accidentally or on purpose. I owe him or her a debt of gratitude I cannot repay, so I'll simply thank the Lord for an earthly treasure that turned up at just the right moment to put my spiritual life on course.

My Bible reading began immediately, and I was well aware of the fact that there was something very special about this journey I was undertaking. I was determined to get through the Bible no matter how tough it might be; and I felt good about it. Though I had found the time to read books for pleasure plus books required in both high school and college, I had never found time to read the entire Bible. At 42, I had never even felt a need to do that. Suddenly, I had a reason. I prayed that my reading would forever put to rest the question our pastor had asked me that morning: "If you died today, do you know beyond a shadow of a doubt that you will be saved?"

With God's help, I joined a miniscule group of those who have read His Word from cover to cover. Perhaps most important, I read the Bible as Martin

Luther had done more than 500 years before me. I read it with only the wisdom of the Holy Spirit. Because Luther chose to leave his Catholic doctrine behind and read the Bible on his own, he was moved to vehemently challenge the earthly church to which he had been doctrinally devoted. The Holy Spirit led Luther on a journey he could never have imagined. Luther changed generations of people who believed they had to earn their way into heaven. He stood against the Catholic Church, the most powerful instrument on earth at that time. If Luther could read the Bible and change the world, I could read it, too.

Each day, my Bible reading began with a prayer that the Holy Spirit would be my guide. Then, I read all the information in the "Bible Pathway" pamphlet regarding the history of the time, who wrote the excerpt, and so on. Naturally I began in the book of Genesis. Early on, I was relieved to learn that the first five books of the Bible—the Jewish Torah—gave me few new insights (or at least that's what I thought at the time). I have to admit that I came away with a great appreciation for the daughters-in-law of Noah, who left parents, siblings and extended families to die and followed their father-in-law in faith. I asked myself if I could do that and later taught the enormity of that decision in my Adult Bible classes. From the standpoint of the teacher in me, I was amazed to read the book of Deuteronomy because it is a review of the first four books. A good review of material can be a powerful tool on the way to successful learning, and God used that tool to perfection in His book.

I loved every minute of my daily reading. I learned some new things and was reminded of things I had previously learned. I was happy that I was finally doing what I knew I should have done a long time ago. I was so committed to this project that if I was going to be gone one day and knew I couldn't read the Bible, I read ahead so that I wouldn't get behind and make an excuse not to continue. It was all about commitment. Months passed, and I was moving right along. Little did I know, though, what was just ahead—and worst of all, I wasn't the least bit prepared for it.

CHAPTER 5

HISTORY FROM YESTERDAY FOR TODAY AND TOMORROW

As I read the Old Testament, problems continued to grow for me with regard to my relationship with my church. These issues were especially clear as I began the book of Ezekiel where God speaks of His terrible judgment on Israel for their sin. In Ezekiel 11:16, the Lord tells the Israelites: "Although <u>I have scattered you in the countries of the world</u>, I will be a sanctuary to you during your time in exile. <u>I, the Sovereign Lord, will gather you back from the nations where you are scattered, and I will give you the land of Israel once again</u>." Thanks to my tenth grade world history teacher, Mr. Sylvester, who took our class to see the movie "Exodus," I knew the Israelites returned to their beloved homeland in 1947, fought a war, and reestablished the nation of Israel in 1948. I loved that movie and could vividly recall scenes from it as I read the book of Ezekiel. (Isn't it amazing that a public school teacher could, in the early 1960s, take students to see such an excellent movie—one that would never leave me and would be part of my book one day? That couldn't happen today, could it? We've left God out of our schools and look what has happened to them).

God would reiterate His promise to return the Jewish people to their homeland in Ezekiel 28: 25-26: "This is what the Sovereign Lord says: 'The people of Israel will again live in their own land, the land I gave to my servant Jacob, for I will gather them from distant lands where I have scattered them. I will reveal to the nations of the world my holiness among my people ... and when I punish the neighboring nations that treated them with contempt, they will know that I am the Lord their God." This was a profound statement to me. God spoke to Ezekiel about "the nations of the world." Just think how little that meant to Ezekiel at the time. How big do you think the world was in the eyes of Ezekiel? Yet, God knew He wasn't writing those words just for Ezekiel but for those, like me, who would live to see the nation of Israel restored. I never would have known this had I not read the Word. Suddenly, halfway through the Bible, I watched the history of my lifetime unfolding in a book that had been written thousands of years before. I was mesmerized, but it would be the next book of the Bible that would change my life forever.

The book of Daniel follows Ezekiel. Through my church, I had, over the years, learned all about Daniel ... or so I thought. Here is what I knew: By God's grace, Daniel survived a night in a lions' den. His friends Shadrach, Meshach, and Abednego survived a toss into a fiery furnace; and Daniel had been the only person who was able to successfully interpret King Nebuchadnezzar's dream. I remembered all three of these stories from my earliest years in Sunday school. Daniel had even become a hero of mine. It was exciting to read the first six chapters, which were a review of the stories about Daniel that I had loved as a child. Then I got to chapter 7. Nothing would ever be the same for me again.

Unbelievably, Chapters 7-12 of Daniel contained information I had never heard before despite 40 plus years of membership in the Lutheran Church and two years at a Lutheran university. I remember the feeling of disbelief and even betrayal that I felt about my church as I moved from word to word and chapter to chapter. For whatever reason, I began to believe my church was involved in a "great deception." This was exactly what I hoped I'd never face—the idea that the church of my heritage was not teaching the entire Bible. Suddenly, I was faced with the question: Why? I remember thinking, "There must be a good reason; perhaps this is an isolated incident." I told myself not to jump to conclusions. Still, the pain of this discovery would not go away. Even worse for me was the fact that there was nothing difficult to understand in these final chapters of Daniel.

I had always believed that pastors took this difficult Bible and helped me understand it because I wouldn't have been able to understand it any other way. Momentarily it crossed my mind that I may have heard this so that churches could retain absolute control, but my heritage forced me away from such thoughts. I did not want to believe it because it was just too painful.

Chapters 7-12 of Daniel simply represent visions Daniel was given by God in regards to the end of the world and the second coming of Christ. For the first time, I could see both history and daily events foretold in the Bible thousands of years earlier. I was dumbfounded! No one had ever spoken to me about "End Times" before. I was told that Jesus could come at any time. Of course, that is basically true. He could claim me today in death. In Daniel, I learned, though, that there actually is a plan for the end of the earth, and not everyone knows it or sees it because they haven't read about it or because their churches—like mine—don't teach it. As I completed the book of Daniel, I found that I could watch the Bible come to life as I read the newspaper. I could listen to the news on television and say, "I read about that in the Bible!" How exciting! At the same time, I also realized that not everyone could do that. I had been given a gift—a gift *available* to everyone but one which only a few would receive because the majority simply trust the church to teach the "truth." The majority of people, like me, have been indoctrinated.

Or, was I wrong? Might my church have a valid explanation for not teaching the entire Bible? That certainly was my hope, and I owed it to the church to speak with my pastor regarding what I had read. I knew I would do that when my Bible reading was complete.

Though I didn't know it at the time, Daniel 7:9-10 discussed heaven and God the way I saw it in Ezekiel and would eventually see it again in Revelation. Verses 11 and 12 are actually found in Revelation. Verses 13 and 14 tell us about Jesus and His authority at the end of time. That description continues in verses 23-28. Daniel 8:23-25 is a foretelling of II Thessalonians and Revelation 13, and that foretelling continues in Daniel 11. Daniel 12 would jump right back into my memory when I got to Thessalonians and Revelation. God gave Daniel the same vision in the Old Testament that the Apostle John received in the New Testament book of Revelation. Both of them would be given this vision so that you and I, after reading our Bibles, would know God's plan for the future beyond a shadow of a doubt. For the generation who would live to see His plan accomplished, God would bless those who had read and were aware. I believe God will also use those who are aware as witnesses and comforters when those dark days come.

At this point in my reading, not only did I begin to see God's plan unfold for the end of the age as we know it, but I also began to see His unending love and devotion for the nation of Israel. In the book of Amos, God sends His wrath upon nations that do not support Israel. I had been taught by my church that "Israel" in the Bible does not mean the nation itself but the church of believers. As I continued to read the Bible, however, I began to believe that is false teaching. God is very clear—always—throughout His Word that the nation of Israel is very dear to Him. He also makes it clear that the rest of the world will one day pay a terrible price for mistreating the nation God calls His own. In Amos 9:8-15, we read: "I, the Sovereign Lord, am watching this sinful nation of Israel and I will uproot it and scatter its people across the earth. Yet I have promised that I will never completely destroy the family of Israel," says the Lord. "For I have commanded that Israel be persecuted by the other nations as grain is sifted in a sieve, yet not one true kernel will be lost......In that day, I will restore the fallen kingdom of David. It is now like a house of ruins, but I will rebuild its walls and restore its former glory. And Israel will possess what is left of Edom and all the nations I have called to be mine.....I will bring my exiled people back from distant lands, and they will rebuild their ruined cities and live in them again......I will firmly plant them in the land I have given them, says the Lord your God. Then *they will never be uprooted again.*" After reading this, how can anyone see the church as "Israel"? God speaks directly about the *land* of Israel, not His church. He repeats the promise made in both Ezekiel and Daniel that though He was scattering the Jews, he would one day restore their land, bring them back to it, and never uproot them again.

God began the fulfillment of this promise in 1947 when the Israelis came back after World War II, where they were nearly exterminated; fought for the land they believe God gave them; and became a nation in 1948. In recent years, the Jewish people are coming back to Israel in caravans—some returning by air from Russia and Africa. I am astounded at the fulfillment of God's promises. God's plan has been available for thousands of years for all mankind to see and know—written clearly in His Word. But because I, and most of you, have clung to the teachings and traditions of our churches and haven't read the Bible completely for ourselves with just the Holy Spirit as our guide, we have missed the best God has for mankind—the final chapters of *His story* (do you see the word "history" here?).

I was now eager to read more and struggled every time I had to put the Bible down. The words of the prophet Zechariah would contain the next major revelation God had for me. Written 500 years before Christ, Zechariah speaks about this Jesus who would come and will also come again. I learned that "on that day, His feet will stand on the Mount of Olives east of Jerusalem and the Mount of Olives will be split in two from east to west," and people will flee through the valley that is created. "Then the Lord my God will come and all his holy ones with him" (Zechariah 14:5; compare with I Thessalonians 4:14). Those who are in heaven with the Lord at the time of His return will come back with him "on that day." What an incredible revelation! My parents and grandparents, my brother and nephew, my brother-in-law, my aunts, uncles, cousins, and all those who came before them and were saved—even me, if death has taken me before then—will return with the Lord to be a part of His final victory over sin, death and Satan. I had never heard that before. How about you? Won't that be a marvelous day? I was slowly becoming convinced of my salvation.

Zechariah continues in verse 6, "The sources of light will no longer shine yet neither will there be continuous day. There will be no normal day and night, for at evening time, it will still be light. On that day, life-giving waters will flow out from Jerusalem, half toward the Dead Sea and half toward the Mediterranean … On that day, the Lord will be king over all the earth. On that day, there will be one LORD—his name alone will be worshiped.... And Jerusalem will be filled, safe at last, never again to be cursed and destroyed. And the Lord will send a plague on all the nations that fought against Jerusalem ...The wealth of all the neighboring nations will be captured." (Zechariah 14:6-14).

I had just read another book in the Bible about God's promises at the end of time. Most of all, I learned, once again, that God expects nations to support the nation of Israel. Those who do not will be punished. How is it that I didn't know a thing about this? What caused my church to reject forever so much of the Bible? The greatest surprise was still ahead for me, though. The words of the prophet Zechariah would be repeated in the New Testament. My Lutheran pastor had said that if you find something in the Old Testament and again in the New Testament, it is fact. Too bad he later forgot those words, as you will soon see.

The final book of the Old Testament—Malachi— brought another surprise: I had never known tithing is an edict from God. What is "tithing?" It is the giving of the first 10 percent of your income back to God. It isn't an idea; it's a requirement. I had always thought it was simply an idea originating from man to keep the church successful. Beginning in Malachi, chapter 3, verse 8, I read, "Should people cheat God? Yet you have cheated Me! ... You have cheated me of the tithes and offerings due to me. You are under a curse, for your whole nation has been cheating me. Bring all the tithes into the storehouse ... If you do, says the LORD Almighty, I will open the windows of heaven for you. I will pour out a blessing so great you won't have enough room to take it in. Your crops will be abundant....Then all nations will call you blessed, for your land will be such a delight," says the LORD Almighty." Wow! What an enlightening moment when I read that! God doesn't simply *suggest* we give 10 percent. He says we *rob* Him if we don't do that. He also states that He has placed a curse on those nations that rob Him. Any chance there is presently a curse placed by God on America—a blessed nation that has clearly fallen away from Him? When did you last give 10 percent to your church or to a charity in His name? What are you waiting for?

While growing up, I remember that people often complained about the stewardship sermons. Congregational members believed that giving to the Lord was their personal business. They could give what they wanted to give, and no one should tell them differently. What does the Bible say about this, however? First of all, stewardship is not simply about the giving of money. It is also about the giving of one's time and talents. Since we have a free will, God doesn't beg us for our stewardship gifts. What He does tell us in Malachi is that if we don't give 10 percent of our income, we have robbed Him.

People who don't read their Bibles think sermons about giving are for the bounty of the church, and churches often don't use the money wisely. I can't argue with that, but there are many ways we can honor God with our tithes. Besides giving to the church, there are many charities that desperately need resources. Our gifts to them also honor God. Just think what churches could do for God if they didn't have to worry about simply paying bills; and, if all Christians gave a tithe, churches would flourish. America is faltering because it has not honored God, and we have not honored God because we don't read His Word and follow His directives. We never really got to know God. We had a *head* religion in our denominational church but not a *heart* relationship with Him. The fault doesn't lie with God. It lies with us.

Shortly after I read about tithing in Malachi, my husband suggested we begin to give God 10 percent of our income. There was now no doubt in my mind that we were to do that, but I couldn't imagine how we would meet our bills if we did. We had three children to raise and many needs yet to be met. Like everyone else, we had financial obligations. Doing what is right in the sight of God is not always easy—in fact, it's often painful, but I knew my husband was right. We began to tithe.

It wasn't long before we watched a miracle take place. We actually witnessed God's promise in Malachi acted out in our lives. God did, indeed, "open the windows of heaven" for us, and He continues to do so to this day—some 20 years later. We never cease to be amazed. God keeps His promises. When we are weak, He is strong; and when we obey, He blesses us. We've never missed one penny of our tithe, and our financial blessings, as well as other blessings, have continued to far exceed anything we could have imagined. Test God! He's waiting to bless you.

Malachi is placed in the Bible, in my opinion, in the perfect spot for a final look at the Old Testament. It gave me a great deal to consider. First, it taught me that tithing is a requirement of God and not a choice.

Though Paul says that "God loves a cheerful giver," that doesn't mean that if we aren't giving cheerfully, we are then exempt from tithing. It simply means we are to tithe cheerfully, and God will bless us.

Second, Malachi presents a warning to pastors and priests. He tells them what their duties are: Not to lie or cheat, live good and righteous lives, guard knowledge, and <u>pass on the truth they received from God</u>. This final statement stunned me and forced me to ask myself: From where had the church of my heritage received the truth—from God or from its synodical leaders? My church would argue, I'm sure, that synodical leaders have the truth. After having read the entire Bible several times now, however, I no longer believe that. They only know what others have told them, and they believe that it's the truth. This is a stark reminder to me of my students and the Constitution assignment I gave them.

Malachi continues the words from God to the priests of that day, "Your guidance has caused many to stumble into sin." Wow! I began to wonder what God would say to the pastors and priests of today. Has their reliance on doctrine over the Bible caused many people in their congregations to stumble into sin? The doctrine of denominational churches has been passed on for centuries and believed without question. Why, after all, would anyone who loved and honored their parents question their parents' religion? If it took me more than 40 years to question, why would anyone else question? This severe warning in Malachi, however, certainly gave me cause for concern for all those who are leading congregations in my denominational church and in all churches everywhere.

Third, in Malachi, God speaks of marriage and those He calls "faithless." God states in Malachi 2, beginning at verse 14: "You cry out, 'Why has the Lord abandoned us?' I'll tell you why! Because the Lord witnessed the vows you and your wife made to each other on your wedding day when you were young. But you have been disloyal to her, though she remained your faithful companion, the wife of your marriage vows. Didn't the Lord make you one with your wife? In body and spirit, you are His. And what does He want? (He wants) Godly children from your union. So guard yourself; remain loyal to the wife of your youth. 'For I hate divorce!' says the LORD, the God of Israel. So guard yourselves; always remain loyal to your wife."

What does this say to America where the divorce rate is 50 percent? I don't see God playing games here! People mock marriage, and churches allow them to do it. People always want to feel good. Obviously, however, God is not that interested in your happiness or mine. He is interested in our holiness. Life is short; eternity is forever. God hopes you'll be happy, but He is more concerned that you are holy and pure. God blesses those who work through difficult marriages in obedience to Him rather than those who take the easy way out.

Unfortunately, people believe that life is theirs to operate as they see fit, but it doesn't matter what anyone believes. It only matters what is written in the Word, and few people have a clue about what is there because they haven't read it. God wants obedience to Him and not obedience to the whims of our lives. Our short stay here on earth isn't about us and our happiness. It's about others, us, and eternal life. God is the judge of how we have lived our lives, and none of us will escape that judgment. What's more important before God—a short and happy life here or eternity?

Finally, like other prophets before him, Malachi discusses the end of the world—the sorrow for those who choose not to follow God and the joy awaiting those who believe in Him, obey Him, and repent of their sins to the end.

Amazingly, I had now finished reading the entire Old Testament and was more than halfway to my goal of reading the Bible in a year. I felt both thankful and concerned. God had broken down myths for me about the difficulty of reading Scripture. Like a movie, He had described the lives of those who have gone before me and had made them real people to me. He discussed earthly places that I had read about and showed me His protection and His punishment. Most of all, He opened my eyes in regards to the earthly church that I had depended upon. The question I asked in the beginning—How do I know my pastor is telling the truth if I never read the Bible?—was becoming clearer and clearer. The answer is that I didn't know—I really didn't know—and you can't know either if you haven't checked your pastor's or priest's sermons against God's Word. To do that, you have to know the Word. To know it, you have to read your Bible.

Part II

"My people are destroyed for lack of knowledge"—Hosea 4:6

CHAPTER 1

THE BRAND NEW "GOOD NEWS"

As I began to read the New Testament, I was confident these final steps to the end of the Bible would be relatively pain-free for me—even though I had many lingering questions for my pastor about the Old Testament. I had rarely missed one Sunday of church in my life, and every Sunday we read from the Bible there—chiefly from the New Testament. So, I felt I was ready to reread it, and I would probably learn very little. How wrong I was! I found information in the New Testament I had never heard before. Perhaps it's time you discover if that's true for you, too.

As this book continues, obviously I cannot "read" the Bible for you. That is your job. As Hosea said, however, the lack of knowledge of God that is found only in the Bible is destroying mankind. I see that destruction more and more every day. Man has failed to read the only book that matters and has made rules for himself about God that feel good to him. This has spared mankind discomfort and the need to confront anyone. In the process, mankind is blind to a world that is dying spiritually because of biblical illiteracy.

In Part II, I will highlight areas of the New Testament that I never knew as well as those parts I never fully understood. I pray that if you are as surprised as I was about what really is in the Bible, you'll feel both a need and a desire to read the Bible yourself in its entirety. If the Holy Spirit accomplishes that in your life through this book, my prayers for you will have been answered.

The four Gospels—Matthew, Mark, Luke and John—began my journey through the New Testament. I had learned during Adult Bible Study classes that Matthew was a Jew writing to the Jews. Mark was a Jew living in Rome at the time he wrote his Gospel and was writing to the Gentiles. Luke was a physician—a Greek—the only known Gentile author in the Bible. I have been told and have read that Luke, not originally a Christian, researched the faith to prove his wife's newly-found faith wrong. Luke's research, however, brought him to faith in Christ, and he eventually became a friend and companion of the Apostle Paul. Bible scholars believe Luke also wrote the book of Acts, which follows the Gospel of John.

John was the beloved disciple. His entire Gospel tells us that Jesus is God and that eternal life will come to those who believe in Him and trust Him for salvation. John was eventually exiled to the island of Patmos where God gave him a "revelation" of His plan for the end of the world as we know it. That "revelation" became the last book of the New Testament. God wanted to show me that plan, and He wants to show you that plan, too. All we have to do is study His Word.

I enjoyed reviewing the Gospels, but it wasn't long before I realized that the Gospels contain far more information than I had ever heard in church before. Again, I was learning that my church was not teaching me and my fellow believers everything we should know, and it was not always accurate in what it defended as truth.

Perhaps my greatest surprise came when I read Luke chapter 8 verses 1-3. I always knew Jesus had selected 12 men He called disciples to travel with Him and to teach so they could eventually "go into all the world making disciples of all nations...." The story of those disciples was taught over and over again from childhood through adulthood in the church. You can only imagine my shock, then, as I came to Luke chapter 8 and learned something I never heard once in my 45 years in the Lutheran Church—and I believe that the majority of you may never have heard this either.

Beginning at verse 1, Luke writes: "After this, Jesus traveled about from one town and village to another proclaiming the good news of the kingdom of God. The Twelve were with him <u>and also some women</u> who had been cured of evil spirits and diseases: Mary (called Magdalene) from whom seven demons had come out; Joanna the wife of Cuza, the manager of Herod's household; Susanna; <u>and many others</u>. These women were helping to support them out of their own means." So, many women, not just men, traveled all around Israel with Jesus. I was absolutely shocked by this. Why would my church and many other churches never mention this fact? Is there any chance that such a revelation would make women question not only the role of women in the church but also why this was never taught or even mentioned?

It appears to me that Jesus had more respect for women than the church hierarchy has had for centuries. I now believe that women have been relegated to positions in the church beneath their dignity, insight, and intelligence because the church has perhaps purposely hidden this information from its members over a lifetime. Is that, perhaps, one of the reasons I was told that the Bible is too difficult to read? The *Life Application Study Bible* explains the verses this way: "Jesus lifted women up from the agony of degradation and servitude to the joy of fellowship and service. In Jewish culture, women were not supposed to learn from rabbis. By allowing these women to travel with Him, Jesus was showing that all people are equal under God."

Though my intense reading of Scripture does not allow me to believe that women should be pastors, elders or deacons, I believe they have a role to play in the life of the church that is much greater than many pastors and priests have allowed. My most pressing question of denominational churches is: While I was a member of a denominational church for 45 years, why was I never once told about these verses in Luke? I believe all women in the church deserve an explanation, but the reality is that churches have been more dismissive of women than God or Jesus ever was. God appointed Deborah as the leader over Israel, and Jesus traveled with women—something many churches have, to date, been silent about. What is their explanation? I believe it's time churches acknowledge something they have totally ignored in the Bible.

The 23rd chapter of Matthew addresses something my Catholic and Jewish friends should consider. Jesus is speaking to His disciples about the teachers of the law and the Pharisees. Verse 7 says: "They love to ... have men call them Rabbi. But you are not to be called Rabbi, for you have only one Master and you are all brothers. And do not call anyone on earth 'father', for you have one Father and He is in heaven. Nor are you to be called 'teacher' for you have one Teacher, the Christ." To my Catholic brothers and sisters in Christ, why have you called the priests in your church "father" for a lifetime when that is forbidden by Jesus in the Bible? Priests, why have you allowed such a title when it is contrary to Jesus' teachings? I ask the same question of those of you who practice the Jewish faith. Your answer will probably be that you don't believe Jesus is the Messiah. Even so, I have to wonder if the traditions of the churches or synagogues are more important than the edicts written in the Bible. Jesus said we are all brothers. There is only one Master, one Father, and one Teacher.

John 16:2 is undoubtedly one of the most revealing things I found in the Gospels. Jesus says in this verse: "A time is coming when anyone who kills you will think he is offering a service to God." Those words, written thousands of years ago, sent shivers down my spine. When I hear people say, the Bible is 2,000 years old and is no longer relevant, I immediately think of this verse and the people who died on September 11, 2001, as well as those who have died at the hands of terrorists all over the world. What do these terrorists believe? They believe that they are serving Allah, their god, by killing Christians, and they believe that dedicated service will bring them a reward of many virgins.

The Bible predicted the time in which we're now living—from the very words of Jesus who obviously knew about 2001 more than 2,000 years ago. He spoke the words and John recorded them for all of us to read. How relevant, then, is the Bible? If one verse predicts so much, how can anyone say it isn't relevant to our time? Here's another question: Is Allah and the God of the Bible the same, as many believe? They cannot possibly be because the God of the Bible is a Triune God—Father, Son and Holy Spirit—and Allah is a single god. A Triune God and a single god cannot be the same God.

One of the greatest misrepresentations and downfalls of the Christian church, I believe, is found in Matthew 7:1 and in Luke 6:37. This is what Christians call the "do not judge" verses. These verses tell us not to judge others or we, too, will be judged. Sadly, though, because we Christians don't read the entire Bible, we have missed the other part of these verses. So, we have escaped the Great Commission Jesus left for us: To witness to one another. In order to witness, we have to "judge," don't we? I cannot possibly witness to anyone unless I first decide he or she is not a Christian or is not behaving as a Christian should. In doing so, I have judged them, and, heaven forbid, we don't want to do that, do we? So, we breathe a sigh of relief that we don't have to really, in the words of the old hymn,

"Stand Up for Jesus." Phew! We don't have to witness! Let's see, though, if that is true.

Go forward from Matthew and Luke to Corinthians 5:11. Paul is writing to the Christians in Corinth to correct serious problems he sees among church members. He writes: "You must not associate with anyone <u>who calls himself a brother</u> but is sexually immoral or greedy, an idolater or a slanderer, a drunkard or a swindler. With such a man, do not even eat." We cannot follow these directions from God through Paul if we don't first judge the person, can we? If we do follow these directions, aren't we labeling (judging) them? Doesn't that violate the verses in Matthew and Luke that have protected the church from witnessing requirements for 2,000 years? Let's continue reading at verse 12 and see. Paul writes: "What business is it of mine to judge those <u>outside</u> the church? Are you not to judge those inside? God will judge those outside. (But) expel the wicked man from among you." What is God, through Paul, saying here? He is telling us that we are not to judge the ungodly; that is God's job. It is our *duty*, however, to judge those who call themselves Christians. What might this say to the Catholic Church who for years protected priests who molested young boys, were transferred, and then went on to molest even more? God says, "...expel the wicked man from among you." The hierarchy of the Catholic Church has obviously been disobedient to the Word of God for years.

How have you and your church fared in this edict from God? Have you taken the easy road and said to yourself or others, "I can't judge that person" or have you realized that the word "judge" in Matthew and Luke means those outside of the church and not those in the church? How has your church explained this? Until I read the Bible myself, I only heard that I cannot judge. How about you? The church has used the Matthew and Luke verses to give you and me an "out" from witnessing, but when has Jesus given us that "out?" He left His work—witnessing—first to the disciples and then to us, and we've leaned on the "do not judge" words as an escape. We only "escape," though, until He calls us to heaven where He'll ask us if we carried out The Great Commission. How will you and I answer Him?

In Matthew 5:10-16, Jesus tells us that we are the "salt of the earth." Salt adds flavor to life, doesn't it? Yet, salt can also sting. I love Florida, and one of my favorite things to do there is swim in the salty ocean. When a wave catches me off guard, though, I sometimes come up from under its grip with a mouthful of salt water. That is not a pleasant experience. In the same way, God never intended us to enjoy witnessing or the recipient to enjoy hearing what we have to say. God simply requires us to do it. In that context, He sometimes asks us to be "salt" to someone where Jesus is concerned. Sometimes our words for Jesus may sting another person. As tough as that is, God will always give us the tools to accomplish what He asks us to do.

In a November 8, 2009, television sermon, the late Dr. D. James Kennedy said in regards to witnessing, "Jesus didn't call us to be 'sugar.' He called us to be 'salt.' He didn't call us to be vinegar, either. Salt makes us thirsty." And in a December 27, 2009, note to his congregation, Pastor Tim Iseringhausen of Christ

Lutheran Church in Bexley, Ohio, wrote the following: "Jesus came to comfort the afflicted and *afflict the comfortable.*" Sometimes we are "the comfortable" and sometimes "the comfortable" are others. Are you aware just how difficult it is to witness to "the comfortable?" They either appear to have no need for Jesus or they believe they are saved and are "comfortable" in that position, even though salvation may not be theirs.

It is often said that the toughest people to witness to are those firmly planted in denominational churches where they are "comfortable"—often due to heritage and tradition. Pastor Iseringhausen, though, tells his congregation that Jesus came to "afflict the comfortable." Is it our job as Christians, then, to simply leave people in "comfy" situations, or should we "salt them"—whatever the risk—knowing that eternity is more important than any short earthly relationship we have with them? You and I both know the answer to that. The question is: Will we take a risk for Jesus? Is that a choice or did God say witnessing is a requirement that has no choice? I believe the latter is true. Let us all, then, pray that we offer "salt" in our witnessing and that we make someone "thirsty" for Jesus. That is the way it is supposed to be. Be honest now—just how much "salt" have you been shaking into the world for Jesus?

Speaking of witnessing, one of my favorite witnessing tools is that of the transfiguration found in Luke 9:29. Jesus took his disciples up on a mountain to pray. "As he was praying, the appearance of His face changed, and His clothes became as bright as a flash of lightening. Two men, Moses and Elijah, appeared in glorious splendor, talking with Jesus. They spoke about Jesus' departure, which He was about to bring to fulfillment at Jerusalem... As the men were leaving Jesus, Peter said to Him, 'Master, it is good for us to be here. Let us put up three shelters—one for you, one for Moses and one for Elijah.' While Peter was speaking, a cloud appeared and enveloped them and they were afraid as they entered the cloud. A voice came from the cloud saying, 'This is my Son whom I have chosen; listen to Him.' When the voice had spoken, they found that Jesus was alone."

In 2005, when my mother was on her way to heaven, she asked me if she would know her birth mother there. When my mother was two, her birth mother died, and she was raised by her maternal aunt and uncle. Though mom had a wonderful life, she yearned to know her birth parents. In asking this question of me, I believe she hoped that she would meet them in heaven but was also troubled as to whether or not they would actually know one another. My answer was that she absolutely would know them, and I used the transfiguration to explain why. The disciples knew Moses and Elijah even though they had never seen them before. One might argue that Jesus told the disciples what would happen before Moses and Elijah appeared, but that is not what the verses say. We are told in verse 29 that "Jesus took his disciples up on a mountain to pray." Clearly, that is all they knew. Why did Jesus' appearance change and why did Moses and Elijah appear? In my opinion, that happened so the disciples would believe beyond a shadow of a doubt that there is a heaven where people receive glorified bodies and live forever. And when

Jesus died and ascended, they would be assured of who He is and where he is.

"Yes, Mom," I said, "You will know your birth mother, she'll know you, and we will all know one another. Jesus promised us that in the transfiguration."

I have also used the story of the transfiguration in my witness to Jehovah's Witnesses. They believe heaven is only for 144,000 of them, and to get there, they must work to earn a spot. They have no explanation for me, however, when I speak to them about the transfiguration. It is, I believe, at the core of our assurance that heaven exists and is a place where we will know our loved ones. The Jehovah's Witnesses don't have that assurance. What a blessed assurance of eternity the transfiguration is for those of us who have read the Bible ourselves and know about it.

Whenever we witness, it is important to remember to witness to children. They are Jesus' future disciples. I remember one interesting moment with children when I was teaching Vacation Bible School to fifth graders many years ago. A discussion arose about some sibling rivalry taking place in the home of a young boy in the class. I explained that Jesus knew all about that kind of thing because he, too, had brothers and sisters living in his home with Mary and Joseph. The boy, with much skepticism in his voice, wanted to know how I knew that. I told him that it's written in the Bible (good thing I knew where to find it because he challenged me immediately on that). We opened our Bibles to Mark 6:3 where the names of Jesus' earthly brothers (James, Joses, Judas and Simon) appear. That verse also states that Jesus had sisters, but they aren't named.

The boy and others in the class were amazed, and I thought it was sad that these children got to fifth grade without knowing something as simple as that. They were even more amazed to learn that Jesus' brother James wrote the book in the Bible of the same name. The biblical book of Jude is believed to have been written by another of Jesus' brothers.

Chapter 6 of the book of Mark teaches us more about Jesus than I imagined. The setting of this chapter is Nazareth, the town where Jesus lived and worked in his father's carpentry shop. It was the Sabbath, and Jesus and the disciples and the women with Him went to the Nazareth synagogue where Jesus began to teach. The town's people were amazed and said, "Where did this man get these things? What's this wisdom that has been given to Him that He even does miracles? Isn't this the carpenter?" They took offense at him. This didn't mean a lot to me until I saw a DVD done by Rob Bell, pastor of Mars Hill Bible Church in Grand Rapids, Michigan. Not only was I fascinated by the video, but I actually visited Pastor Bell's church to ask him how he had discovered the information in the video. I then searched the Internet myself and learned much about early Jewish history.

At the time of Jesus, Jewish boys memorized the Torah under the direction of the local rabbi until they were ten years old. The boys were then separated into two groups. The rabbi selected "the best of the best" to continue studying with him, which was the next step in becoming a rabbi themselves. Those not selected returned to their villages to learn the trades of their father. Think now. What happened to Jesus? Are you astonished to realize that Jesus—God's Son—was not selected by the rabbi as "the best of the best." I certainly was. Jesus, our Savior, had not met the mark. How do I know this? I know Jesus wasn't chosen as a future rabbi because the Bible tells us in Mark 3 that the village of Nazareth recognized Him as simply a carpenter—the trade of his father, Joseph—and when Jesus was 12, he was so busy astonishing the teachers in the temple in Jerusalem that His parents lost Him. Jesus was clearly living at home in Nazareth with His parents and was not studying at the feet of the rabbi. Jesus was not chosen by an earthly church leader as "the best of the best." Wow! What does that tell us about the wisdom of those early Jewish church leaders?

Now let's go back to the people of Nazareth. Is it any wonder that they were shocked to hear Jesus in the village synagogue and took offense at him? After all, they all knew He had not been chosen by the local rabbi as one of the boys who had talent enough to be a rabbi. So, why was He teaching in their local synagogue? Who did He think He was? Mark 6:6 says it all: "He (Jesus) was amazed at their lack of faith." The Nazareth locals were so caught up in the rituals of the Jewish system that they missed their Savior. A young boy not chosen by an earthly rabbi because he wasn't "the best of the best" came to earth to save them from their sins, but their earthly beliefs and traditions kept them from seeing and knowing the truth. That nearly happened to me. How about you?

Are you so caught up in the rituals, traditions, and doctrine of your church that you, too, have missed the Savior, even though you're certain you haven't? Have you read the only book God left for you to read, or are you relying on your church to teach the Bible their way to you?

Jesus said to His disciples as he was selecting them: "I chose you; you did not choose me." Do you now understand the significance of those words in the hearts of 12 men the local rabbi had not chosen and who were sent back to their villages to be fishermen like their fathers? These "ordinary" men became forever famous, while the rabbi's "best of the best" neighborhood boys would die as "ordinary." Jesus takes the ordinary and makes them extraordinary.

What about when the disciples heard Jesus' words: "I will make you fishers of men." Isn't that what the rabbis were supposed to do? I now see the miracle that the disciples saw when Jesus chose them. He removed the synodical blinders from their eyes. Have those same synodical blinders been removed from your eyes?

The most intriguing moments in the reading of the four Gospels were the chapters entitled "The End of the Age." A new reality in Scripture for me is that God has a plan—a definite plan—for the end of the world as we know it. I first saw the plan in the book of Daniel and was shocked to get more information about it in the Gospels. Paul shares even more about it in his writings, but the book of Revelation brings the plan together and allows us to see what is ahead in our lives. I am choosing to skip "The End of the Age" information found in the Gospels for now and will share it later when I discuss the book of Revelation. I believe you will be as shocked as I was about the information God has for us in the Bible in regards to

His final plan for mankind. I would have missed it had I not read the Bible for myself because my church didn't, and still doesn't, teach it. Have you missed it? More importantly, *will* you miss it?

The Gospels contain mountains of information we all should know such as: We cannot hate our brother but must love our enemies; we must forgive others or we are not forgiven; we are to do good deeds in secret; worry is a sin; we must acknowledge Jesus publicly before men or He will not acknowledge us before His Father in heaven; there is no marriage in heaven; we are not to make oaths but simply let our "yes" be "yes" and our "no" be "no." Jesus says that anything beyond that comes from the evil one (Matt. 5:33-36), and there is only one unforgivable sin—blasphemy against the Holy Spirit. If you were unaware of these things, the Bible will make them clear as you read it.

We need to consider one final thing as we conclude our New Testament study of the Gospels. This is the assurance that Jesus is alive—now and forever. In Luke 20:27-38, the Sadducees ask Jesus questions about marriage. He tells them that there is no marriage in heaven and (those in heaven) "can no longer die, for they are like the angels. They are God's children since they are children of the resurrection." Jesus then goes on to say, "But in the account of the (burning) bush, even Moses showed that the dead rise, for he calls the Lord 'the God of Abraham and the God of Isaac and the God of Jacob.' He is not the God of the dead but of the living, for to Him all are alive." Jesus lives and has been alive for more than 2,000 years. His Gospels show me a living, loving, forgiving director of our lives now and forever. I was, and still am, so grateful for all I learned in my reading, but the best was yet to be.

CHAPTER 2

THE CHURCH GROWS— HAVE YOU?

Frankly, as I began to read the books of Acts and Romans, I had little motivation for those books. In fact, I was hoping to get through them rather quickly and move on. For whatever reason, I was never very interested in the formation of the early church, the basic purpose of the book of Acts. My attitude was quickly transformed, though, when I realized that this book tells Christians what it takes to follow the Great Commission that Jesus left for us. It allows us to see that, despite what we believe, we can all do what the apostles did to spread Christianity—not because we are capable but because the Holy Spirit will come upon us if we ask Him to and will give us the courage, wisdom, and strength to witness, as He did for the disciples.

At a September 2008 crusade in the state of Kentucky, the speaker, Steve Hale, head of the Steve Hale Evangelistic Association of Woodstock, Georgia, stated that 97 percent of Christians will go to their graves having brought no one—**no one**—to Christ. Imagine that! Such a statement both shocked and saddened me and gave me great concern for the first meeting we will have with Jesus after our deaths. We don't think about that enough. If we are among the 97 percent who have witnessed to absolutely no one, how will we explain that to Jesus since that is the job He left for us to do? Will He accept our excuses that we were too shy or we didn't want to offend or judge anyone? Will He accept our excuses that we were simply too busy working two jobs, raising children, caring for aging parents, coping with illness, and more? You and I both know the answer to this—Jesus won't accept *any* excuse. He placed us here to do His work. Everything else is secondary, not vice versa. He gave us a lifetime to witness. Yet, one day, we will have to stand before Him and we'll see how many souls we walked by who are now in hell. Father, forgive us, and fix our priorities so that we are not among that 97 percent. What a shameful percentage in the life of the church!

If we read Acts carefully, it is an amazing story. Jesus told the disciples to wait in Jerusalem until the Holy Spirit came upon them. In Acts 1:8, Jesus said: "You will receive power when the Holy Spirit comes on you, and you will be my witnesses in Jerusalem and in all Judea and Samaria and to the ends of the earth." Those were the final earthly words Jesus spoke before He ascended into heaven. Imagine the thoughts of the disciples as they heard the words "to the ends of the earth." How far do you think they thought that was? They could not possibly fathom that their witness for Jesus would one day lead to the true "ends of the earth."

Yet, nothing is impossible with God. Your witness to one person—just one—may indeed take your words to the very ends of the earth. How incredible would that be? The book of Acts begins the story of a witness for Jesus that has, indeed, traveled, as He predicted, to the very "ends of the earth," and Jesus said He would come again after all had heard. How close are we now to that coming?

The Holy Spirit did come upon the disciples, as Jesus said. Peter's marvelous sermon followed and nearly 3,000 accepted Christ as their Savior that day and were baptized. The church then began to grow remarkably and daily. As the church grew, the Jewish leaders undoubtedly saw their power and authority challenged and slipping away. Fear of losing power causes good people to do things they otherwise would not do. The temple guard and the Sadducees arrested Peter and John and put them in jail. The next day, the two were forced to appear before the rulers, elders, and teachers of the law who asked: "By what power or what name do you do this?" Their reply in Acts 3 is beyond belief—even to the Jewish leaders who then commanded Peter and John not to speak or teach about Jesus. Peter and John refused and then, amazingly, were let go. God had protected their witness, and that's exactly what He'll do for us.

Jesus promised that, like the disciples, we, too, will be persecuted for His name. I believe that as far as my lifetime is concerned, such persecution began in the early 1950s when Madelyn Murray O'Hare, a confirmed atheist, made the first claim against religion in public places. Then in 1954, churches were told that they could not mix religion and politics. Does this sound anything like the words of the religious leaders of Jesus' day? Do I believe this will get worse? Jesus said it; I believe it; that settles it. Today in Canada, it is illegal for pastors to speak against homosexuality from the pulpit. What Canada is really asking its pastors to do is refrain from teaching the whole Bible. Will that happen in America? I believe we are only a short time away from that. What do you as a Christian plan to do about it? Will you obey God or man?

The generation before us did little or nothing to fight against Mrs. O'Hare or the issue of the separation of religion and politics. People were taught in their churches, as was I, that you don't speak about either. God will take care of an issue like that. All we have to do is pray about it. Where in the Bible does it say that we are to be silent? Doesn't it say we are to be God's witnesses to the ends of the earth? How can we do that if we aren't His witness even in our own backyards?

Had the churches of the 1950s come together—all denominations working together as one with biblical knowledge and despite their differences—Mrs. O'Hare's policies would not have survived. God's workmen—Peter, John, and Paul—would definitely have stood against Mrs. O'Hare. Why are we such cowards? I know the answer to that, and by the time you finish this book, it's my prayer that you'll know the answer to that, too.

Under the greatest pressure, Christians can speak boldly for Christ because we have been given the Holy Spirit. Every time the disciples and their followers were jailed for speaking on behalf of Christ, the Holy Spirit protected them. Even when they, like Stephen, died for the cause, their death was a witness (see Acts 7). On the day that Stephen died, a great persecution came against the church in Jerusalem, and all but the apostles were scattered throughout Judea and Samaria. Go back to the final words Jesus spoke before He ascended: "You will be my witnesses in Judea and Samaria….." His prophecy was now beginning to be fulfilled. As Joseph once said in Genesis 50:20, what man meant for harm, God meant for good to accomplish the saving of many lives.

Sometimes pain is part of God's plan. He may use you to accomplish His purpose, and pain might be required. God called Sarah Palin to do just that during the 2008 Presidential election campaign. From the very beginning, she stated that she is a Christian and stands on biblical principles. Immediately, the criticism from the liberal media began. God said in His Word that Satan is the prince of this world. Does anyone doubt that after watching Sarah Palin—and even George Bush—seemingly destroyed by the liberal media? I am shocked that even one Christian would vote Democratic. Sarah Palin and George Bush paid a horrendous price for their Christian principles, but they won a victory no earthly person can take away from them. They stood publicly for their God. Would you be willing to endure that kind of ridicule and pain or even a little discomfort to stand up for Jesus or bring a soul to Christ? That is exactly what He, in His Word, requires you and me to do.

I heard a story not long ago that illustrates the point very well. During a service at a large church, two hooded men ran up the aisle claiming to have guns. With the service halted, the men spoke to every person in the church and asked if he or she was a Christian. If they said, "Yes," they were escorted to the back of the church where they believed, I'm sure, that they would be executed. The others were left where they were seated. After all had been asked—and remember this was a large congregation—only 25 members admitted to being Christian—just 25. Everyone else, undoubtedly out of fear of death, had denied Christ. I hope that I would not deny Christ in a situation like this, but the fear of death might—though I pray not—take precedence. Where in that scenario do you think you would be?

The good news is that this entire episode was apparently staged to help Christians see their lack of real faith. Imagine how the people felt in the end when they realized this wasn't real—except for their denial of Christ. I'll bet no one ever forgot that day! Some day God just might ask some or all of us to stand up for Him even in the face of death. Will you and I do that? I pray we will.

Jesus' last earthly words stated that the disciples will witness "to the ends of the earth," and the fulfillment of those words began with the conversion of Saul to Paul. Saul was involved in the destruction of the church. He went from house to house, dragging off Christian men and women and putting them in prison. Does that remind you of the Holocaust? The Bible says, though, in Acts 8:4 that "those who had been scattered preached the Word wherever they went." Nothing would stop what the Holy Spirit began. One day Saul met Jesus on the Damascus road. His life was never the same again. Acts 19:11 says, "God did extraordinary miracles through Paul." That's the way it is when we accept Jesus and do His work and His will.

The early church continued to grow, and missionary journeys around the Mediterranean to witness about Jesus became commonplace. The final chapter of Acts has Paul in Rome in a rented house where he welcomed all who came to see him. The last sentence of Acts says, "Boldly and without hindrance he preached the kingdom of God and taught about the Lord Jesus Christ." I believe that with the Holy Spirit, all of us can say the same thing if we only trust Jesus and give our lives completely to Him. If you haven't spoken boldly for Jesus, what is your excuse? Has Jesus accepted that excuse? Where witnessing is concerned, the toughest moment is the first time you do it. After that, you are so thankful you did what you were placed on this earth to do that you'll want to witness more. Test God on this one; you'll be glad you did.

CHAPTER 3

THE UNVEILING

At this point in my Bible reading, I realized that both Martin Luther and I share a life-changing experience in our readings of God's Word. We both found things that our church had not taught us and other things our church had taken an obviously incorrect biblical stand on. For Luther and me, the words of Scripture led us on paths for Jesus that we could never have imagined. It was clearly the best thing that ever happened to both of us, though in the eyes of God, I am no Martin Luther!

In the book of Ephesians, Luther found the peace he had long sought. He tried everything to find peace with himself and with God. As a devout Catholic, he even became a monk believing that if he cloistered himself, he would experience "the peace of God that passes all human understanding" (Philippians 4:7), but that didn't happen. Nothing Luther did gave him peace until he read the Bible and, in particular, Ephesians 2:8 which says: "For it is <u>by grace</u> you have been saved, through faith—and this not of yourselves, it is a gift of God—not by works, so that no one can boast." This one verse not only gave Luther peace, but it gave him conviction, strength, and determination to challenge the church of his people and his heritage, even though the possibility of death loomed over him in doing so.

At the time of Luther, the Catholic Church was selling indulgences or payments for sin. Church officials would ride through towns and villages on horseback. Residents confessed their sins and the church official would determine a fair price for the forgiveness of those sins. People didn't question that practice. Why would they? It was church law, and what ordinary person had the knowledge to dare question the rules of the church? Ordinary people hadn't gone to seminary; the priest had. After all, the church was only living the rules of the Bible, wasn't it?

When Luther read the Bible and saw Ephesians 2:8, he knew the church was in a sinful state because monetary payment for sin is not a biblical principle. We are saved by grace and not by works. No amount of money given can forgive a man or save a man. Salvation is a gift of God, and Luther then knew the truth—a truth the Catholic Church at the time wasn't teaching and certainly wasn't living. The Ephesians verse led Luther to search and question other teachings of the church. When his heart was at peace, on October 31, 1517, he nailed 95 theses to the door of the cathedral in Wittenberg, Germany.

No one dared challenge the Catholic Church, which was all powerful at the time, not to mention the fact that the church would lose a lot of money if the sale of indulgences were discontinued. Luther's challenge would result in a death sentence for him. He had to know that. Yet, with great conviction and courage, Luther stood up for God. It was God first, religion second, and it always would be.

Amazingly, people who came to believe what Luther believed protected him. By whom were those people sent? Who stood beside the disciples as they witnessed to the world in which they lived? It was, of course, the Holy Spirit. The Holy Spirit protected Luther as well. Because Luther was faithful in upholding God's Word, he was protected. You and I will be protected in our witness, too.

Luther eventually left the monastery, married Katherine, had children, and lived his life, having changed the church forever. One ordinary man standing up for biblical principles was used by the Holy Spirit to change the world. All of this happened simply because Luther loved the Lord and, most of all, read and studied his Bible. In doing so, he saw the sin of his church.

The Lutheran Church is today and always has been proud of Luther, as it should be. His challenge of the Catholic Church of old has been life-changing. Luther, however, was not a perfect man. Among other things, he was extremely anti-Semitic. This is well documented. As a Lutheran, I was almost led to worship Luther. Every year Lutherans celebrate Reformation Sunday on the last Sunday in October. At that service, they honor Luther. I often wondered, as a devoted Lutheran, if Luther had a seat in heaven next to Jesus. Today I realize that through the years, Lutherans have failed to recognize what Luther really did. Yes, he changed the course of history and that of the church, but he never would have done that had he not read and studied the Bible. He wouldn't have recognized the sins of his church but would have continued to believe that the church was simply carrying out the edicts of the Bible. Why would he think otherwise?

The Catholics of Luther's day believed wholeheartedly that the Catholic Church's sale of indulgences was biblical or the church would not have been selling them. Had Luther not read and studied the Bible, that practice may have gone on for generations. How many people today can prove their church wrong based on their own personal reading and studying of the Bible? Very few! Even if Luther had, in his mind, questioned such a sale, without reading the Bible, he would have had no proof.

Now let's think about you and your church? Do you know beyond a shadow of a doubt that what your church is teaching is biblical? I doubt it. If you haven't read and studied the entire Bible, how would you know? I believe the Holy Spirit will lead you to question that as you read Part III of this book.

Before we move on, it is important to answer a question many may have in light of the sale of indulgences as a covering for sins. The question is: Are all sins equal in the sight of God? The Catholic Church has separated mortal sins from venial sins for years. Was it right for this church to "sell" forgiveness? Absolutely not. The Catholic Church knows that now. Does the Bible, however, support the equality of sins or was the Catholic Church at least somewhat right in its belief in the inequality of sins? This is a question I hear many Christians discuss.

The answer has two parts. First, as far as salvation is concerned, all sins are equal in God's eyes. Jesus' brother James says in James 2:10: "Whoever keeps the whole law and yet stumbles at just one point is guilty of breaking all of it." That is true. Heaven is a perfect place for perfect people. No sin can be connected with heaven. Sin separates us from God. That is why He sent Jesus. Redemption from sin requires a blood sacrifice, and it is the blood of the Lamb Jesus that cleanses us. "The wages of sin is death." No matter what sin you and I commit, all sin would send us to hell if it weren't for the blood of Jesus and our repentance. If all sins are equal, then, in the sight of God, does He handle them all the same? That is the second part of the answer.

In Hebrews 12:6, the Bible says, "The Lord disciplines those he loves, and He punishes everyone He accepts as a son." Psalm 99:8 says: "...you were a forgiving God to them, but an avenger of their wrongdoings." One thing we know for sure is that God does not ignore sin. He forgives sin that has been repented of, but He still disciplines. Do we recognize God's punishments for sin?

The Bible supports the fact that God does not handle all sin the same, except in the area of salvation. Jesus tells us about that in John 19:11: Speaking to Pilate, He says, "You would have no power over me if it were not given to you from above. Therefore the one who handed me over to you is guilty of a <u>greater</u> sin." Those are Jesus' words about the equality of sin.

What are some Biblical examples of God's punishment for sin? The flood that covered the earth leaving only Noah and his family to survive and the complete annihilation of Sodom and Gomorrah are two major examples that we all know. Are there others? Though faithful Moses led God's people for 40 years in the wilderness on their way to the promise land, he was not allowed to enter that land because he disobeyed a directive from God. The Lord told Moses to *speak* to a specific rock so water would come forth; instead, "he *struck* the rock and the rock was Christ." (Numbers 20:7-12 and I Cor. 10:1). Moses' disobedience and his striking of something that is holy prevented him from crossing into the land with the Israelites. He received an earthly punishment from God. Another good Bible reading on this is Hebrews 10:26-31. God does punish sins on earth, and He punishes those differently. The good news, however, is that if we repent, He forgives those sins.

If we're in tune to God, we will recognize His discipline. That's the purpose of it. I'm sure you've heard the Bible verse, "A man reaps what he sows." (Galatians 6:7) My mother used to say, "You will be paid back for what you do and others will, too. It might be many years before you see that happen, but it will happen." As usual, Mom was right. I have, over the years, seen my sin pay me back and have also watched God discipline others on my behalf.

God's chastisement clearly comes in different forms for different sins. For example, the punishment for speeding can be a hefty fine, so we will think of that ticket and slow down next time. The ticket can be painful. Who wants to give $200 to any city when that money could be used for other things? Once the initial pain of that fine subsides, though, we might remember it, but we aren't tormented by it. If our speeding leads to a traffic accident that kills our neighbor, however, that sin is now a cancer in our mind that lasts a lifetime. The punishment could be many years in prison, far away from those we know and love. Though punishment comes for our disobeying the law, the degree of punishment is different in each case.

Here is one more example for us to ponder: I can easily "kill" someone's spirit with gossip. I can even destroy that person's reputation with words. I would probably be happy at first, or I wouldn't have gossiped so horrifically in the first place. Eventually, though, such an act might remain on my heart long enough to cause me to seek repentance and forgiveness. Then, all would be well. What if I had an abortion, however, "slaying" that tiny baby God created and placed in my womb? Deuteronomy 27:25 says, "Cursed is the man who accepts a reward to kill an innocent person." You may ask, "What 'reward' does one get in an abortion?" The "reward" is freedom. That unwanted child will now not hold a mother back from doing what she chooses in life. Initially, she will probably be happy about it. It has been proven, though, that the majority of women who have had an abortion suffer terribly for it later in life.

Does God punish all sin? Yes. He punishes the sin of unbelief for eternity. He disciplines and punishes other sins on earth—sometimes "to the third and fourth generation of those who love Him." When He does

94

the latter, the punishment always "fits the crime," but He is also always waiting to forgive. Can God forgive one who aborts His child? Yes! God sent His Son to cover that sin as long as it is repented of. That's the good news of Jesus.

One verse in the book of Ephesians forced Luther to see that man cannot "buy" forgiveness for sin from a church because Jesus "bought" us once and for all on the cross. He carried our sins and gave His life so we might live eternally. Luther's eyes were opened by the Holy Spirit through his reading of God's Word. The same thing happened to me. Instead of a verse in Ephesians, it was one chapter in the book of Romans that became my "Luther moment." Nothing in my Christian life would ever be the same after reading Romans, and when I began my reading of Scripture, I simply couldn't have imagined the impact that experience would have on me, my husband, our family, and our future.

According to the *Life Application Study Bible*, Paul wrote the book of Romans about A.D. 57. He was planning a trip from Corinth to Jerusalem with a stop in Rome before going on to Spain. The Gospel message was, indeed, taking him "to the ends of the earth" as Paul knew that "end" to be. The Roman church at the time was composed of mostly Jewish converts to Christianity who had gone to Rome to witness. The church had many Gentile members as well.

Some of my favorite Bible verses and favorite Bible truths can be found in Romans. In the first chapter, Paul says that man is without excuse where faith in God is concerned because, since creation, God's invisible qualities have been clearly seen and understood from what has been created by Him. In other words, even those who have never heard of God are responsible for recognizing that the world didn't just happen, and God will hold them accountable for that recognition or lack thereof. The amazing beauty and incredible functioning ability of the earth and its people is, according to Paul, a faith establisher—no missionary necessary. When people ask the question: What about the man in the bush who has not heard? Paul has given that person and others the answer: God will accept no excuses. We are responsible for what we have seen.

In chapter 3, God, through Paul, repeats what Isaiah had said so many years earlier: "There is no one righteous, not even one … there is no one who does good, not even one … no one will be declared righteous in his sight by observing the law… righteousness from God comes through faith in Jesus Christ to all who believe … for all have sinned and fall short of the glory of God." It is wonderful to think that we're good or that others are good. I know people who never fail to love others and are right there when someone needs them. I have heard some say that because they're good, they'll be saved. I've heard others say "if (he or she) doesn't get to heaven, I haven't got a chance because they're so good." Many, many people believe that "being good" is a heavenly pass. The Bible is very clear, however, that good people don't go to heaven—only perfect people do. Good doesn't mean a thing in the eyes of a perfect and holy God. "Good" is man's measure for heaven. It isn't God's measure. How good does one have to be in the eyes of a perfect God in order to be saved? When can people stop being good and know they're in? How does anyone become perfect enough for heaven?

Heaven is a perfect place with a perfect God, and anything less than perfect doesn't count. God explains to Moses in Exodus 33:19 and Paul repeats in Romans, "I will have mercy on whom I have mercy and I will have compassion on whom I have compassion." The choice is not up to us, and the work is not up to us. How then can we be saved? That is the very question the disciples asked Jesus. Jesus responded: "With man this is impossible, but with God all things are possible." He continued: "You who have followed me will also sit on twelve thrones judging the twelve tribes of Israel. And everyone who has left houses or brothers or sisters or father or mother or children or fields for my sake will receive a hundred times as much and will inherit eternal life." It's not about us, folks; it's all about Jesus.

"Good" doesn't get you the kingdom. In fact, hell will be filled with a lot of good people who forgot to read their Bibles and learn the truth. Jesus shed His blood for us; accepting that premise is the only way to heaven. It is that shedding of blood that saves mankind because God requires a blood sacrifice. "It does not, therefore, depend on man's desire or effort but on God's mercy." (Romans 9:16). Do works matter at all then? They certainly do, but only after faith has led us to Jesus—not one moment before. It is not "Jesus plus" anything. The Virgin Mary can't get you to heaven; lighting candles can't get you to heaven; following church laws and traditions can't get you to heaven; good works can't get you to heaven; forgiveness by a pastor and priest can't get you to heaven. Faith alone, followed by a lifetime of works that display that faith, wins the heavenly prize. As James said in his biblical book: "Faith without works is dead."

I enjoyed reading the verses from Romans 1-10. I had heard so many of those throughout my lifetime. Then I got to Romans chapter 11, and my "Luther moment" began. I will never forget where I was the moment the Holy Spirit freed me from the spiritual blindness I had held forever through the church of my heritage—the blindness that kept me a prisoner from the truth. Like Luther, I would be led to never again totally believe the hierarchy of any denominational church. I learned it is not what any man says— even one who went to a seminary or one who holds a high office in a denominational church. All that matters is what is written in God's Word. Luther and I were now united. We had both found the fallacies of our church in the very best place to find them—our Bibles.

To really grasp what happened to me, you have to read Romans chapter 11 before you continue reading this book. Ask the Holy Spirit to remove from your mind any denominational leanings and let the Spirit— and only the Spirit—show you what he wants you to see in this chapter. Do not read ahead in this book until you have prayed and then read chapter 11. The story of my new life in Christ and my release from the bondage of biblical illiteracy and blind indoctrination will end Part II of this book, and it's a story that I hope and pray will change your life the way it changed mine. Though another area of the Bible would also be profoundly enlightening for me, the real change began in Romans 11, and I can sing without hesitation the words of a Gaither song, "Praise God I'm not the (wo)man I used to be."

Please remember that as I read Romans 11, I was still Lutheran and wanted to remain Lutheran. Though the reading of the Old Testament and some things in the Gospels made me want to sit down with my pastor for clarification, I had no intention of doing anything but finding the answers to my concerns. Romans 11 would forever change that, however.

In chapter 11, the topic is Israel, the country, and not "Israel, the church." At the very beginning of this chapter, Paul discusses the fact that God did not reject Israel, the nation, even while grafting Gentiles into His kingdom. I may need to remind you at this point that the Lutheran Church sees the word "Israel" in the New Testament as the church. According to television evangelist Dr. Jack Van Impe, this is due to "Replacement Theology." For 431 years, the church taught the 1,000 year reign of Christ. St. Augustine came along and said the world will end and replaced the word "Israel" with the word "church" and the word "Jerusalem" with the word "heaven." St. Augustine's theory was taught in Catholic, Lutheran and Presbyterian churches. Much of the Bible in denominational churches became the Bible according to St. Augustine rather than the Bible according to the Holy Spirit. Without checking, Christians simply believed what their churches taught them; and I was as guilty as the rest. It is interesting that churches teach that every word of Scripture is God breathed, but those churches then come up with new theories and change the Bible's entire meaning.

Romans 11:5 was eye-opening to me. Paul clearly speaks of the nation of Israel in the first four verses and continues in verse 5 by saying: "So, too, at the present time, there is a remnant (of Israel) chosen by grace…. What Israel sought so earnestly it did not obtain, but the elect did. The others were <u>hardened</u>." The word "hardened" jumped right out at me. I remembered that God had hardened the heart of Pharaoh during the escape of the Israelites from Egypt, but the hearts He hardened in this case were those of His chosen people. Was Paul really telling me that God had hardened their hearts? Yes! I know this because of the next few verses: "God <u>gave</u> them a spirit of stupor, eyes so that they could not see and ears so that they could not hear <u>to this very day</u>." I was seeing a mighty tough God there—someone who doesn't play games and not the "Mr. nice guy" people often choose to characterize Him as. He clearly punishes disobedience, sometimes harshly. Israel disobeyed many, many times and God forgave them. Finally, God had enough, hardened their hearts, and gave them eyes that could not see and ears that could not hear the truth.

The real shock came for me, however, in Romans 11:25-31: "I do not want you to be ignorant of this mystery, brothers, so that you may not be conceited" (Ha, ha, Israel; you fell and I got in!). Here, then, came the clincher for me: "Israel has experienced a hardening in part until the full number of the Gentiles has come in. And so, <u>all Israel will be saved</u>." I sat breathless in my chair. This chapter was definitely not about Israel, the church. It was about Israel, the nation—God's chosen people. The Lutheran Church was clearly wrong in its teaching, and I knew at that moment how Luther felt. Unless my pastor could show me exactly why this hadn't been taught to me in 45 years, my membership in the Lutheran Church was over. I had been misled—biblically deceived.

I was even more convinced as I read verses 28-31 of Romans 11: "As far as the gospel (the good news of salvation through Jesus Christ, who the Jews believe is yet to come) is concerned, they (Israel) are enemies on your account; but as far as election is concerned, they are loved on account of the patriarchs, for God's gifts and His care are irrevocable." God loves His Israeli people, and He says without hesitation in verse 26 that "all Israel will be saved"... and that doesn't mean the church; it means the nation. Verse 30 begins: "Just as you (Gentiles) who were at one time disobedient to God have now received mercy as a result of their (Israel's) disobedience, so they, too, have now become disobedient in order that they, too, may now receive mercy as a result of God's mercy to you." God showed mercy to the Gentiles so He must show mercy to Israel on account of their election and the promises He made to them. God keeps His promises.

I had never heard any of this before; and contrary to what I had been taught, there was nothing difficult to understand here. God blinded the eyes of the nation of Israel because of their disobedience, but they would not be blinded forever. He would never revoke His promise to them, but His punishment (notice God's punishment for sin) towards them allowed you and me—the Gentiles—to be grafted into His tree of life. I was reminded of the power of God in two verses in

Luke 24. In regards to Jesus' walk after His resurrection on the road to Emmaus with His disciples, verse 16 says: "But they were <u>kept</u> from recognizing him." Verse 45 says: "Then <u>He opened their minds</u> so they could understand the Scriptures." Was this what God was doing to me? Had He waited for me to find Him and know Him in His Word and then remove the blinders? There is no doubt in my mind that is exactly what He did. The Bible says that when you draw close to God, He will draw close to you. He left me a book to read and waited more than 40 years for me to do just that. Once I read it, He drew close to me and has never left me.

God allowed me, as He may be allowing you, to remain in the blind indoctrination of my life due to illiteracy of the Bible and my attachment to heritage and tradition above all else. I can't blame the church alone, though. I had already had the Bible for more than 40 years, and it had collected dust. I was responsible for what I hadn't read, and I was responsible for my unwarranted faith in my church. The church of my people is still caught in a history of manmade doctrine based on a sketchy study of the Bible. The church, however, doesn't save any of us. In fact, our holding on tightly to what the church teaches rather than our study of the Bible may very well lead to our destruction. Yes, I believe God waited a lifetime for me to read His Word and then, removed the denominational blinders as I read it. He'll do that for you, too. When do you plan to get started?

After reading Romans 11, I read no further that night. Like Luther, my whole world had changed.

Throughout the Bible, I had seen problems with what my church taught, but this was a "three strikes and you're out" moment. My church was smart, though. They didn't teach the parts of the Bible that were the least bit controversial, and, to this day, the majority of Lutheran believers are blind followers. That, I believe, is true in all denominations. The conversations I have had with Christians in denominational churches astound me. People are simply robots of the denomination to which they belong—so much so that they wouldn't consider fellowshipping with a Christian of another denomination, even if the future of our nation depends upon it

The morning after I read Romans 11, I went to my regular Tuesday morning Bible class at the home of my pastor. The study was led by his wife. I had not planned on mentioning what I had read. I planned to discuss it only with my pastor, but something was discussed that morning that led me peacefully and with confidence to share what I had read. The pastor's wife simply said she would relay my concerns to her husband, and he would get back with me. A week passed, and I returned to Bible class. There waiting for me was the answer from my pastor. It was a mimeographed page from the Lutheran *Book of Concord*—the doctrinal position of the Lutheran Church Missouri Synod on Bible verses. I was shocked! What I expected was a biblical explanation or a discussion with the pastor with only the Bible between us. I was no longer interested in a set of position papers from any denominational church on any issue. Was this always the way Lutheran pastors answered the questions and concerns of their congregational members? Was this just the way it was done in my church? Why would any church set the Bible aside and seek answers from a book written by men—no matter how learned— rather than a book written by God?

I read the explanation and became angrier by the moment. The Lutheran Church Missouri Synod still today stands by its belief that the word "Israel" in the New Testament is the "church," and they do that because the hierarchy and pastors either haven't read the entire Bible or they have read it with a denominational bias. By the time this incident occurred with my pastor, I knew the truth, so there was no way that I could discuss the paper with him when my anger ran so deep and was so raw. I clearly saw the unwavering allegiance of mankind to its churches rather than to the Bible.

Martin Luther and I had, for the first time, connected. Though I had admired his heroic stance before, I never really understood what he went through. The agony over his decision to leave the church of his heritage had to be overwhelming. The reality that the church he loved and supported was wrong must have stung. Like Luther, I knew I had taken my first step toward leaving the Lutheran Church and I was in shock. My sister and brother-in-law had left the Lutheran Church about ten years earlier, and I remembered how aggrieved I was by that. How could she do that? After all, she was leaving the church of our heritage. But, of course, I came to understand exactly why she left. The Lord had simply spoken to her heart before He spoke to mine. Little did I know that she had been praying a long time for me to have the same experience she had.

My husband, a Lutheran all his life, was unaware of my newly found insight. I certainly couldn't leave the church without him. What about our children? How would this affect them? All I could do was pray. I decided to begin to share with my husband and continue reading God's Word to the end. Then I would see what we were led to do.

Luther tried first to reform his church by nailing 95 theses to the door of the Wittenberg church. I don't believe he meant to leave the church but only reform it. His 95 theses' posting was met with disdain and the real threat of death. He must have been shocked. He had served the church with his whole heart, but God was telling Luther that that was the problem—he had served the church but not the God *of* the church. Luther, like me, had put a church ahead of God. The church was, then, according to the Bible, my idol, and God speaks of His disdain for idols: "Thou shalt have no other gods before me." My church and its teachings had become my god. I had placed my family traditions and my German heritage above God and blindly followed. I felt that, like Luther, I would soon have to take a bold step. It would take courage to do that, but I began to "see the forest for the trees." Lutheranism had, at that moment, been taken out of my heart and soul. I was sad and disheartened, but little did I know the plans God had for me and my husband as the future unfolded. To some extent, even today, I can't believe what happened in our lives. I can only praise God for it.

CHAPTER 4

RULES FOR LIVING—
YOURS OR HIS?

As I continued my journey through the New Testament, I became enthralled with the very first overseer of churches—Paul—and the difficult assignment God had given him. The disciples at the time were transforming Jews, Gentiles, and atheists alike into believing Christians who were eager to serve God. They were doing so, however, in a world that didn't share their views and had ideas of its own about the gods that should be served. Sound familiar?

For generations, American churches have stood as a beacon of hope with a set of biblical guidelines that kept our society orderly. Those guidelines, however, have been whittled away and watered down by those who now choose to live as they please and write their own Bibles that allow them to live as they decide, while challenging the Bible written by God. Some even loudly declare that "there is no God." The same thing happened in the early church; but God chose

Paul, a reformed Jew, to stand firm for Him, as well as to teach and nurture the new churches. Paul did not make the rules of Christian living he writes about; he simply shared those with the church. The newly-established churches trusted him and followed God's teachings through him. Paul proved that the words he spoke to the churches are God's when he tells his protégé Timothy "all scripture is God-breathed" (2 Timothy 3:16). So, the new converts believed Paul was speaking the words of God (I believe that, too), and the churches flourished under that direction.

Though my parents held me to the standards written by Paul, I didn't really know that those standards are in the Bible. I simply trusted their wisdom and lived life as they directed. As adults, we are to live by the wisdom of God that we learned first from our parents, but our knowledge of God should increase as we read His Word for ourselves. As I continued to do that, I was genuinely surprised to learn that the rules my parents taught me actually are in the Bible. I'm now able to appreciate what they taught even more than before.

One of the things my mother stressed over and over again as she shared with me how she and my dad expected me to live is: "I won't ever see everything you do. I couldn't possibly do that; but God is everywhere and sees everything. If what you do is something you can do with God watching, go ahead and do it." No other words of my parents kept me on the right track as much as these. It's true that God is omnipresent—everywhere at the same time—and sees everything. One day, we will have to account for all those "everythings," even the ones we thought we got away with. I'm thankful we have a forgiving God, but He only forgives what we truly repent of. We have to remember that His grace is neither easy nor cheap. He exchanged His own Son for that grace.

Paul, as God's spokesman, didn't mince any words in his letters to the new churches. When he heard of a problem or witnessed a problem, he tackled it in truth and love. He didn't make excuses nor did he tiptoe around an issue. As I read his "God-breathed" words, I see why our society today is in trouble. By far the majority of people both living and dead have never read the entire Bible. For the most part, they believe what their churches teach—if they go to church—or they write a set of rules that suit them. Paul warned against such things. The problems society faces today are written about and solved in the Bible, but how would you know that if you haven't read it?

The entire middle section of the New Testament was written by Paul from the book of Romans through the book of Philemon. In each of these books, the Holy Spirit, working through Paul, taught mankind how to live, believe, worship, and witness following the death and resurrection of Christ. Paul laid the rules of God out in simple and reasonable fashion. Mankind doesn't need a pastor or priest to interpret Paul's books for him or her, despite what we might have been taught. Why would God write a book that mankind wouldn't be able to read? He wouldn't. After all, He is holding us to the precepts He teaches there. He can't possibly hold mankind responsible for words they can't read or understand.

First and Second Corinthians was written to teach Christians how to live in a corrupt society. Like today, the new Christians of Corinth wanted to fit in, be liked, and be accepted rather than stand up for Jesus and rise above evil. They loved Jesus but found it too difficult to be different as God calls us to be different. False teachers also continually undermined the church and the teachings of God, causing problems for the new Christians. Despite it all, Paul never wavered from God's truth. Unfortunately, that isn't happening today. Churches everywhere in America are fitting into society rather than rising above it, and our society is going against the Word of God because churches are not teaching that Word in its entirety. Paul's written exhortations deplore such actions.

As I continued my reading, I was amazed at the rules God (not man) established, yet society (even Christians) mocks God and does what *it* thinks is right. I first saw that in I Corinthians, chapter 6. Paul writes that one Christian is not to sue another Christian. I wonder how many Christians know that. He states that Christians will one day judge angels; therefore, we surely should be able to settle lawsuits among ourselves rather than go to unbelieving judges or non-Christian juries for the settlement of disputes.

In Matthew, Jesus tells us exactly what to do when we have difficulties with our Christian brothers or sisters. First, we are to go to him or her and discuss the problem. If that doesn't work, we are to return a second time but bring one or two others along as witnesses. If that doesn't work, we are to tell the church. If he or she still doesn't listen, the church is then to treat the person as a pagan. Few churches are holding its people to these teachings of Jesus. Who is willing to take a tough stand these days?

Paul wrote that lawsuits between Christians are not only a bad witness, but they also are often settled by unbelievers who don't share our Christian values. Does that mean we should never go to court? Absolutely not. A non-Christian won't settle a dispute with a Christian in a church. In that case, our legal system has to be used, and we have to go there in the hopes that God will still be glorified. If, however, the Christian is going to court for vengeance, that is sin. Romans 12:19 says, "Do not take revenge but leave room for God's wrath, for it is written: 'It is mine to avenge; I will repay,' says the Lord." If you feel wronged even after a court case, leave it with the Lord and know that He will handle it. He promised to do that for you in the book of Romans.

Later in chapter 6, Paul addresses the issue of sexual immorality in a way that I had never heard before. Society today—even some who call themselves Christians—have excused sex before marriage as well as homosexuality. Neither excuse is valid in the eyes of God, and Paul makes that very clear. Through Paul, the Holy Spirit tells us in I Corinthians 6:9: "Do not be deceived. Neither the sexually immoral nor idolaters nor adulterers nor male prostitutes nor homosexual offenders ... will inherit the kingdom of God." Paul continues in verse 13: "The body is not meant for sexual immorality but for the Lord and the Lord for the body ... Do you know that your bodies are members of Christ Himself? Shall I then take the members of Christ and unite them with a prostitute? Never! Do you not know that he who unites himself with a prostitute is one with her in body? For it is said, 'The two shall become one flesh.' But he who unites himself with the Lord is one with him in spirit. Flee from sexual immorality. All other sins man commits are outside his body, but he who sins sexually sins against his own body. Do you not know that <u>your body is a temple of the Holy Spirit</u>, <u>who is in you</u>, whom you have received from God? <u>You are not your own</u>; <u>you were bought with a price</u>. <u>Therefore, honor God with your body</u>." Wow! All I can say is "thanks" to my parents and to my husband's parents who taught us to refrain from sex until marriage. I am thankful that I loved and trusted my parents because though they believed this, they didn't read it to me from Scripture. I'm sure they learned right from wrong from their parents who learned it from their parents. Though my husband and I honored our parents and, most importantly, God and were, therefore, abstinent, I wish my parents had read this passage to me from the Bible. I believe if more Christian parents used the Bible instead of their own words to guide and direct their children, our society could be different.

Why is sexual immorality rampant today? There are many reasons but the greatest of them, I believe, is that people have walked away from Bible truths. Sadly, though more than 90 percent of Americans say there is a God and 80 percent of them say they are Christians, only 38 percent are Bible-believing Christians. According to Bob Schiefer of CBS News, June 29, 2008, 70 percent of believers say that Jesus Christ is not the only way to salvation even though

Jesus Himself said, "I am the Way, the Truth and the Life. No man comes to the Father except by Me" (John 14:6). If you claim to be a Christian, however, and ignore these things, you aren't a Christian at all—no matter what you claim.

Revelation 3:16 says: "Because you are lukewarm—neither hot nor cold—I am about to spit you out of my mouth." Heaven was not made for fence sitters or those who choose to write their own Bibles. It was created for those who believe, repent, and turn from their evil ways. You can't be a Christian and follow the ways of the world or your own belief system. That concept is simply a well-orchestrated plan of Satan. Remember Satan's words to Eve in the Garden of Eden: "Did God really say, 'You must not eat from any tree in the garden?'" When Eve replied that she could eat from any tree but one or she would die, Satan said, "You will not surely die.... For God knows that when you eat of it your eyes will be opened, and you will be like God, knowing good and evil." You know the rest of the story. Do you really think Satan has changed from then until now? In reality, he is leading mankind through the evil world of sexual immorality exactly as he did when he purposely misled Eve; and America might as well be called "Eve" because it has fallen for Satan's lies just as surely as Eve did.

At a Wayne County, Kentucky, Christian crusade in September 2008, Steve Hale of Georgia gave the following statistics: 50 percent of today's young people are sexually active; 48 percent of boys and 33 percent of girls are sexually active by age 15. They have had seven sexual partners by age 18. Every 67 seconds, a teenager has a baby and will have another one in two years. One out of four teenage girls has a sexually-transmitted disease. The first sexual experience for a teen occurs between the hours of 3 p.m. and 6 p.m. in his or her own home when the parents are at work.

At a Save Sex conference I attended in Michigan, the speaker gave the following reasons why teens have sex: To be popular, peer pressure, they believe it's safe with a condom, everyone is doing it, curiosity, they feel grown up, because they're drunk, because they want to get pregnant, rebellion, or on a dare. What few have told them is that people can and often do die from illicit sex, but absolutely no one dies from virginity. More importantly, the Bible says that if you're a Christian, your body is the temple of the Holy Spirit; and when you have illicit sex, you are doing that with God present. One day your name, as well as mine and that of every person living today, will appear in the obituary section of our local newspaper. On that day, you will meet God. Please explain to me how you will then explain away your sexual transgressions. How many parents are using the Bible to teach their children, or are we simply letting Satan, who the Bible says is the prince of this world, have his way?

Paul says in I Corinthians, chapter 6 that "you are not your own; you were bought with a price" and, therefore, you are to "honor God with your body." Has any abortion-believing, church-going, Christian-claiming person ever heard of those biblical words before? If not, they are, according to Paul, still "without excuse." The people of America who are screaming for a "woman's right to choose" need to tell me how they will justify that to God on the day they meet Him in death because, according to Him, "your body is not your own"—no ifs, ands, or buts about it!

Abortion is not acceptable in the eyes of God. Jeremiah 1:5 says: "Before I formed you in your mother's womb, I (God) knew you." A Psalm of David states in 139:13, "You created my inmost being; you knit me together in my mother's womb. I praise you because I am fearfully and wonderfully made ...<u>your eyes saw my unformed body</u>. All the days ordained for me were written in your book before one of them came to be." David knew God was the creator of life and Job said, "The Lord gives and the Lord takes away." Mankind was given a free will to believe anything he or she wants to believe. If you want to believe Satan's lie that abortion is okay, you are free to do that; but that freedom ends the day you die, when your judgment comes. Feel free to then explain to God why you destroyed or supported the destruction of one of the children He created simply because you believed, against the teachings of the Bible, that a woman has a right to choose. God's way or your way—which will get you to heaven? Perhaps the words of Jesus might help: "Not everyone who says to Me, 'Lord, Lord' will enter the kingdom of heaven, but only he who does the will of my Father.... Matt. 7:21.

Almost unbelievably, more babies have been aborted in America to date than all men and women killed in all wars. That is astounding! In fact, according to Heritage House of Taylor, Arizona—one of the largest providers of pro-life material in the country—44,044,600 babies have been aborted since Roe vs. Wade became the law of the land on January 27, 1973. Heritage House sells an envelope sticker that equates that number to the loss of the entire population of the states of Oregon, Idaho, Montana, North Dakota, Minnesota, Iowa, Nebraska, Wyoming, South Dakota, Nevada, Utah, Colorado, Kansas, New Mexico, Arkansas, Oklahoma, Alabama, and Mississippi. If someone came to America today, bombed those states and killed every person there, you and I would be horrified and would fight against such slaughter, wouldn't we? Well, that is exactly what happened to babies in our country. Where have you and I been? More than 44,000,000 babies to whom God had given special talents for the betterment of our nation and our world were disposed of. Abortion doctors: Look out for God. He's coming back. He said in the Bible: "I will repay."

Those of us who call ourselves Christians are aware of the abortion slaughter and, in many cases, have either looked the other way or have justified it. How can any of us call ourselves Christians and support the annihilation of God's creations? America shutters, as it should, at the extermination of six million Jews murdered by the Nazis in World War II (as the Germans and much of the world looked the other way), and we are glued to our TVs when a beached whale might die if it can't be returned to the sea or pelicans are covered with oil in an oil spill; but we look the other way at the more than 44 million babies—humans and God's creations—who have been aborted. How can that be? Is there any wonder why God seems to be judging America?

We all grieve, as we should, for each and every one of those American servicemen and women who gave their lives so we might be free, but we care little or nothing about the intentional death of a baby, often murdered by brutally vacuuming that God-created child piece by piece, limb by limb from the womb until he or she is fully extracted, at which time his or her head is punctured if the baby is still alive. How barbaric is that! Man says that practice, called partial birth abortion, is a woman's right to choose. God says women have no right to choose since their "bodies are not their own; they were bought with a price." Perhaps if more people read their Bibles, fewer babies would be aborted. I personally "choose" to be on God's side. How about you?

Even church-going Christians support abortion. On August 8, 2008, Fox News reported that House Speaker Nancy Pelosi stated that she, an ardent Catholic, studied church history and learned that before 1533, the church didn't believe life began at conception. Well, Mrs. Pelosi, and others like her, who gives one iota what any church believes? There isn't a Catholic priest or pope or a pastor anywhere who is going to save anyone. None of us are excused from God's wrath because of what our church does or does not teach or believe. Each of us is responsible for knowing what the Bible teaches and living it, and if the Catholic Church before 1533 wasn't teaching God's Word, shame on them! The question still remains: Mrs. Pelosi, why do you claim to be an ardent Catholic and not have a clue what the Bible used in your church says about abortion? Whose fault is that—the church's or yours? And, what right does anyone have to follow a principle that isn't written in the Bible?

The late Dr. D. James Kennedy relates a wonderful story of a discussion he had with a man following a sermon in which Dr. Kennedy had taken a definitive stand on God's Word in regards to abortion. The man was insulted at Dr. Kennedy's anti-abortion stance. Dr. Kennedy said to the man, "So, you believe in abortion." "Yes," the man answered. "Do you also believe in capital punishment?" Dr. Kennedy asked. "No," the man said. "Here's where you and I differ," Dr. Kennedy continued. "You believe in taking the life of the innocent and sparing the life of the guilty, while I believe in sparing the life of the innocent and taking the life of the guilty."[1] What a great answer.

What purpose did God have for that innocent baby who was brutally murdered in the supposed safety in the womb of the one person a child is supposed to be able to fully depend upon—his or her mother? Why doesn't every mother think about the loss society would have felt if they themselves had been the aborted child? Imagine God's pain at mankind's selfish and self-centered abortion decisions. When asked, Dr. Kennedy never backed away from the truth of God's Word. That is exactly what God asks of all of us. The problem is most people don't know God's Word well enough to share it. Whose fault is that?

That is apparently true of even our newest President. Amazingly, Barack Obama sat in a church for 20 years—by his own words, a Christian church—and yet supports a woman's right to choose. He honors his pastor Rev. Jeremiah Wright as a dear friend. What has Rev. Wright taught during those 20 years? Either Rev. Wright hasn't taught it, Obama hasn't gotten it, Rev. Wright hasn't read the Bible, Obama hasn't read the Bible or, even worse, neither accepts the Bible's words as truth from God. Whatever the situation, no Christian can be lukewarm or worldly and be saved. I didn't say that—Jesus did! A friend to the world is an enemy of Christ. What President Obama hasn't realized is that sitting in a church weekly for a lifetime doesn't save anyone, and God doesn't care what we individually believe unless it is in sync with His Word. President and Mrs. Obama support "choice" and yet tell the entire world that they are Christians. What, then, does the word "Christian" mean? Obviously it doesn't mean the same thing to God as it does to the Obamas. Is it possible that even they haven't read the entire Bible, and they, too, live by a Bible they want to believe? I think that is very possible.

Does Nancy Pelosi or President Obama or do you have any idea what the Bible says? Will they and you still be held accountable for a position that is pro-abortion? There is no doubt about that! Wake up, Christians. This life isn't about what you'd like it to be; it's about the way God designed it and wrote it to be. None of us are so important that we are allowed to make society's rules. God judges nations harshly who don't follow His rules. His history of doing that is amazing—and it's all in His Word. If your church isn't teaching God's rules and holding you accountable for them, why are you attending there?

No church has stood more firmly against abortion than the Catholic Church, and they are to be commended for that. Unfortunately, every time I hear them speak about the topic, they always say, "The church says you can't..." or "the pope says you can't." Absolutely no one should care what any church or church hierarchy thinks unless what they say is biblical. In this case, the stand the Catholic Church has taken is biblical; but, where is the praise and honor for this stand going? It is going back to the church itself. I never hear them say, "The Bible says or God says..." They say, "The church says..." It is important for churches to teach people that the church is not the authority on earth; God is the authority. It is not what the pope says, a priest says, a pastor says, a church's leadership says, or what any other church member says that matters. Satan has done a great job of blindsiding mankind to that.

Besides the fact that I believe all people are created by God because He says so in His Word, I also have a personal stake in the abortion arena. My dad was 39 and my mom was 37 when I was born. They had a son, 15, and a daughter six weeks shy of 12. They wanted only two children—a boy and a girl—and were perfectly happy with the two they had. My dad was only a few years away from retiring and fulfilling his dream of moving to Florida. The last thing they wanted or needed in their lives was a new baby. Yet, in the winter of 1945, they learned that they were expecting me. My mom went to three doctors in hopes that the words "you're pregnant" were wrong. I clearly inter-rupted my parents' lives, plans, hopes and dreams. My mother told me that she wasn't happy to be pregnant and didn't want me. Guess what? I fully understand that. What my mom didn't think about at that time, however, was that my birth wasn't up to either her or my dad. God had a plan for my life, and He chose Mom and Dad to be my earthly parents. Perhaps His plan was for me to write a book about Him. I believe it was. Abortion would have stopped that plan dead in its tracks.

Thank God I was born in 1945. In today's society, it is very possible that my mom—if she were not a devoted Christian—would have eventually found a doctor who sympathetically would have provided her the opportunity to abort me. One visit to his or her office, and I would have been history. Thank God my parents were Christians. Thank God I was given life. I believe I had a right to be born and to live. That is my God-given right. I am part of His plan. My parents had nothing to do with it. I believe I had a right to enjoy childhood, endure hardship, find a career that I loved, marry, and have three beautiful children and grandchildren. My parents who were given life by God didn't have the right to take that gift of life away from me. Since 1973 when Roe vs. Wade became law, every living person has had a chance to be aborted—<u>every</u> person. Why weren't you aborted? How would you feel today if you knew your mother had considered that? Do you think she had a right to get rid of you? Or do you feel, like me, that my right to live and contribute to society should never have been taken?

Now, for the rest of the story. Whenever my mom told me she didn't want me, she went on to say that I was a real blessing in her life and in the life of my dad. You see, God had a plan my mom couldn't see in the anguish of an unwanted pregnancy. As I said, she and my dad wanted two children, and that is exactly what they ended life with. Sadly, my brother and his son were killed in a plane crash in 1959. That left my parents with just two children—my sister and me. At the time of the plane crash, my sister was married, and I was 13. My mother told me that my presence in her life and the life of my dad forced them to go on after the loss of my brother. They had someone else to think about other than themselves and their sorrow. God knew that was going to happen, so He created me. What plan did God have for each child who has been aborted? God did have a plan, you know. He tells us that in His Word. What will those who have had abortions tell God about their plan that usurped His plan? Death cannot be avoided; murdering His child can be. Have you repented of an abortion?

How very grateful I am that I had two wonderful, God-loving, God-fearing parents as well as a loving extended family. I am blessed. The Declaration of Independence states that I and every other American have "a right to life, liberty and the pursuit of happiness." I firmly believe that. That right wasn't given to me or anyone else by our founding fathers. They simply knew the Bible and made sure that right would be mine forever (or at least that's what they thought).

God will punish America for what it has done to His unborn children. You can mark my words on that one. He will punish every nation that supports abortion. Life's not about what we want but what God wants for us. Here are some God sayings from the Bible that you might want to remember: "A man's steps are directed by the Lord. A man's ways seem right to him, but the

Lord weighs the heart. In his heart a man plans his course, but the Lord determines his steps. The eyes of the Lord are everywhere. The fear of the Lord is the beginning of wisdom." Obviously, those who believe in abortion don't fear the Lord, so they are lacking wisdom.

Besides "a woman's right to choose," Paul also addresses the sin of homosexuality; and that is exactly what God calls it—sin. Through Paul, God says that no sexually immoral person who is unrepentant shall enter the kingdom of heaven. Mankind everywhere is excusing homosexuality. Again, I ask, who put man above God? In Leviticus 20:13, God says: "If a man lies with a man as one lies with a woman, both of them have done what is detestable." Romans 1:26 says, because of their sin: "God <u>gave them over</u> to shameful lusts. Even their women exchanged sexual relations for unnatural ones. In the same way, the men also abandoned natural relations with women and were inflamed with lust for one another. Men committed indecent acts with other men and received in themselves the due penalty for their <u>perversion</u>." I didn't say these things; God did. When I repeat what God says, I'm not homophobic. I am simply a Christian who has read the Bible and knows what God says in it.

God called homosexuality "detestable," "shameful," and a "perversion." Mankind, however, feels sorry for homosexuals, believing they were born this way. The Bible says, "God <u>gave them over</u> to shameful lusts." Homosexuality is not inborn. God does not purposely condemn anyone to hell. Many ministries have been successful in turning people away from homosexuality.

Why, then, does it continue? Because man has accepted what God condemns. Man is running the show. Even churches are ignoring the Bible. A Lutheran Church in Chicago ordained a lesbian clergy. The Episcopal Church has a homosexual bishop. Why are churches allowing open sin? The truth is they haven't read the entire Bible God wrote and, instead, have decided to write their own.

America, as well as many other countries in the world, operates on the "bible of tolerance." According to the bus driver on our 2008 Cape Cod tour, a well-known resident of the Cape has said that the motto on Cape Cod is: "Live and let live." That is fine if someone is a non-Christian, but where in the Bible do we find that philosophy for a Christian? Nowhere. The Bible says absolutely nothing about tolerance. The idea that we have to be tolerant is simply another ploy of Satan. In Jude verse 23, it says that we have to love the sinner but hate the sin. Where do you see tolerance there? According to the Bible, it is not acceptable for me as a Christian to do anything but love the person who is a lesbian or homosexual, though I do not have to, and absolutely should not, accept that lifestyle. I must condemn the sin while loving the sinner. That's biblical.

In their zeal to serve God, well-meaning but wrongly motivated Christians often step over the line in dealing with things like homosexuality and abortion. It is definitely not biblical to kill an abortion doctor to prevent an abortion, but it is okay to vehemently protest his actions. All murder is sin. True tolerance comes only when sin is recognized, repented of, and not repeated. Don't forget those words: "Recognized, repented of, and not repeated." Jesus gave us that example when He told the woman at the well who had five husbands and was living with the man who was not her husband: "Go and <u>sin no more</u>." Once sin is repented of, and an obvious effort is made not to repeat the sin, I and my fellow Christians can be tolerant. Until then, it is up to us to stand on God's Word by loving the sinner and openly and vehemently hating the sin.

In chapter 7 of I Corinthians, Paul addresses the topic of Christian marriage. In summary, here is what God, through Paul, says about marriage and divorce. A wife must not separate from her husband; but if she does, she must remain unmarried or else be reconciled to her husband, and a husband must not divorce his wife. He also says that a woman is bound to her husband as long as he lives; but if her husband dies, she is free to marry anyone she wishes as long as he belongs to the Lord. Paul said that we are not to be unequally yoked; but if we marry an unbeliever and that spouse wants to leave, we as believers are not bound in that circumstance. As we look at our divorce rate in the United States, how many Christians have held to these God-breathed words? Very few. Why is that? First, it's because Christians haven't read the entire Bible. Second, it's because they hear "the church says..." and correctly feel that the church isn't always right so they're free to decide for themselves. That is where the problem comes in. The earthly church isn't always right because it's led by sinners just like you and me, but the Bible says that Jesus never changes. He is "the same yesterday and today and forever." (Hebrews

13:8). Once you know what Jesus says about marriage and divorce, I think it is wise to heed his directives. After all, the Bible says that the fear of God is the beginning of wisdom!

Let's see how Jesus and Paul compare in their feelings about marriage and divorce. In Matthew 19, the Pharisees asked Jesus if it is lawful for a man to divorce his wife for any reason. Jesus says, "I tell you that anyone who divorces his wife <u>except for marital unfaithfulness</u> and marries another woman commits adultery." He adds in Mark 10: "And if she divorces her husband and marries another man, she commits adultery." Neither the husband nor the wife is given any "out" here. Jesus then says to His disciples, "<u>Not everyone can accept this teaching but only those to whom it has been given</u>." What, then, are the excuses for divorce where Jesus is concerned? Only marital unfaithfulness. That's it. People argue that abuse is a reason for divorce, but what does Jesus say? God says through Paul that people can separate for abuse as long as they don't divorce and remarry. Separation often heals difficult marital situations. In the end, all that matters is what God says.

Being a Christian isn't about how we "feel." It's about faith and the wisdom we receive from God in His Word. We can make all the earthly excuses we choose, but there is only one judge of mankind. You and I aren't that judge, nor is the church. Each of us will have to explain those excuses to God—the one and only judge. So, make your divorce excuse a good one! Churches fail their parishioners in this area. Many correctly tell people they can't divorce but often forget to tell people that it isn't the church that makes this rule (though churches do make rules that aren't biblical). It is God who makes the rule. Pastors/priests should, in **all** circumstances, open their Bibles and show couples what God says. What a failure this has been on the part of churches, certainly in my lifetime. I believe and have seen the rewards people have received from God for their faithfulness to their marriage vows despite lives that haven't always been easy. Now is the time to repent of a divorce due to selfishness, and remember: Repent means "not purposely repeated."

The awakening I felt via the rules of Corinthians would continue, though more softly, from Galatians to Revelation. Much of what is written in these books are important things for me to remember to help me confidently go from day to day, with all its joys and sorrows, knowing that God is aware of it all and will be there for me each and every day of my life. Galatians tells me not to be a slave to the law but be free in Christ. Ephesians reminds me that I am saved by grace through faith and shows me how to be a good wife and mother. Philippians tells me to rejoice in the Lord always—even in the most difficult times and, at those times, to think of good things remembering that I can do all things through Christ who strengthens me. Timothy lays down rules for deacons and teaches us to be kind and caring to widows and older people. I Timothy 5:8 says: "If anyone does not provide for his relatives and especially for his immediate family, he has denied the faith and is worse than an unbeliever." If God came today, how have we cared for those God gave us—those we call "family?"

Timothy also tells us to rebuke sinners publicly so that others may take warning, and the love of money is a root of all kinds of evil. "Some people, eager for money, have wandered from the faith and pierced themselves with many griefs." I Timothy 6:10. Titus emphasizes having Godly leadership in the church, and Philemon speaks about Christian love and forgiveness. Hebrews is a wonderful book about our origin of faith and emphasizes the faith of the Old Testament saints.

One of my favorite New Testament books is the book of James. Written about 49 A.D. by the earthly brother of Jesus, I was mesmerized by his words. James was raised with Jesus; he must have marveled at this man whom he called "brother." He knew Jesus in a way many others did not. Who knows us better than our parents and siblings? They watch all of our personality traits develop and observe the person we become. Because James is Jesus' brother, I accepted his words with ease (how I wish, though, that he had also written an autobiography of Jesus!). James was actually a leader in the Jerusalem church after his earthly brother Jesus ascended into heaven.

James began his book by teaching us that we can handle any trial that comes along in our lives because "the testing of your faith develops perseverance. Perseverance must finish its work so that you may be mature and complete, not lacking anything. If any of you lacks wisdom, he should ask God ... but when he asks, he must believe and not doubt." Who could know this better than James? It is he who says that "every good and perfect gift is from above." God does not bring bad things into our lives; Satan does. God sends

127

perfect gifts, but He does allow problems in our lives so that we may grow. He also disciplines us—and when has discipline ever felt good?

James emphasizes that faith alone is not sufficient and, thus, sets the stage for the Book of Revelation and its judgment of our works—something I never knew would happen to me before I read the entire Bible. James explains that if you believe in God, that's good, but even the demons believe that ... and shudder. He continues: "A person is justified by what he does and not by faith alone. As the body without the spirit is dead, so faith without deeds is dead." I hope many of you who call yourselves Christians are shuddering in your boots at these words of James. Why have so many denominational churches failed to teach this?

Churches, evangelists and loving people who win souls for Christ often make a mistake that causes Christians to stumble. They teach that faith alone in Jesus Christ saves us, and it is there that they stop. So, people believe that faith is all they need. Once they believe this, they go on about their lives with the certainty of salvation. It is absolutely true that faith alone saves. Salvation is all about Jesus and what He did for us on the cross—nothing more and nothing less. Our *first step* in Christianity is faith, but that is not our final step, as many believe. Trouble comes into our lives when we never grow that faith, when we never develop a personal relationship with Jesus, when we never make Him first in our lives, and when we "get" but never "give." Easy salvation, or "cheap grace," as some refer to it, is not acceptable in the eyes of God. He gave us the greatest of all gifts—eternal life. Once we understand the enormity of that gift, we need to do more than simply go to church on Sunday. Going to church fulfills a duty or obligation. That is not what faith is all about. God created us with a purpose, and our focus is to fulfill that purpose daily. To do that, our faith has to grow. Faith and its resulting salvation is only a beginning.

Many denominational churches fail here when they ignore the works part of faith. James tells us that saving faith without works is a dead faith, and his words are supported by the words of Jesus and the Book of Revelation. Does any of this bring to mind the biblical words: "Many are called but few are chosen"? People assume that everyone—or at least the majority of people who die—go to heaven. That is simply not supported in the Bible. I believe that far fewer people are in heaven than we might imagine. Saved people live daily for the Lord, and their works for Him abound, not for salvation purposes but because they love Him so much that they want others to see the Lord through them. Simply going to church every Sunday isn't going to save anyone. Remember, Jesus said lukewarm people will be spit out of His mouth.

James undoubtedly knew the story Jesus told in Matthew 7 about the fig tree. Jesus said, "Every good tree bears good fruit, but a bad tree bears bad fruit.... every tree that does not bear good fruit is cut down and thrown into the fire. Thus, by their fruit, you will recognize them. Not everyone who says to me 'Lord, Lord' will enter the kingdom of heaven but only he who does the will of my Father who is in heaven."

Do you remember the Garden of Eden story? It was built around trees that sustained life and one tree that brought death. In this New Testament story told by Jesus, we are again confronted with trees. These trees are representative of those of us who claim to be Christian. Our works don't save us, but we are to do them as a thank you for what Jesus did for us. If we just accept His death and resurrection and never do anything for Him on this earth, are we truly saved? James says we aren't. James tells us that "faith without works is dead." Jesus told us to share His story with the world, to do good to others, to speak publicly about Him, and on and on. If we don't do that, we are a fig tree bearing bad fruit or no fruit at all. Our salvation is step one, but if we don't serve the Lord following our salvation, our faith is not alive. I didn't say that; Jesus did.

We can't simply be baptized and confirmed and live the rest of our lives with little acknowledgement of a saving faith. We can't step forward for an altar call at a crusade or at the end of a church service and go on the rest of our lives resting on our salvation believing that is all we have to do. Our faith must grow, and the fruits of that growth must be seen by others. We have to take a bold stand for Christ and not simply attend church on Sundays. Does it shock you to know that many who attend church every Sunday have a dead faith? God didn't create us to sit around and enjoy the beautiful earth He created (though that's important, too). He created us to do His will. Jesus said, "Only he who does the will of my Father who is in heaven will be saved." What is God's will for your life? What does He want you to do for Him? Have you asked Him to show you the way? Are you giving the tithe required of you? Are you reading His entire Word? How are you serving Him? Are you following His rules or living by your own? More importantly, what have you personally done to expand His kingdom? Or are you a denominationally baptized and confirmed member of a church who has rested on your laurels and who will face Jesus one day with the shock that what you did wasn't the "work" the Father had planned for you? In the past week, how often have you spoken about Jesus to someone—anyone?

What kind of fruit has Jesus seen on your fig tree? That's the criteria since faith without works is dead. What does that word "dead" mean? Does it mean that we are not saved if we don't have a fruitful faith? Is a dead faith a faith at all? If it's not a saving faith, then those who don't grow and work for the Lord are not saved. James does say in chapter 2, verse 24: "You see that a person is justified by what he does and not by faith alone." Nothing in these words disputes what Paul said in Ephesians about "grace alone." Paul says you can't work your way into heaven because Christ did it all. That is true, but, James' statements occur *after* one has been saved, while Paul's words are before salvation occurs. While works will never save anyone, might the failure to do works to prove one's allegiance after salvation delete that original saving faith? If all Scripture is God-breathed (see also 2 Peter 1:20), are the words of James a warning to all of us who have long held onto the idea that we are "baptized, confirmed and in"? I believe they are, and I also believe denominational churches have failed greatly in this area of Scripture.

Many churches have, in my opinion, given their parishioners a false hope of salvation. The Holy Spirit gives us a saving faith when we believe that Jesus died on the cross for our sins, but He doesn't expect us to then simply go on with our lives. He is waiting for each of us to ask, "Okay, Lord, where do I go from here? What would you have me do for you?" That is the continuation of a saving faith—constantly asking, "What do you want me to do for you today, Lord?" Amazingly, all the good you might be doing for Him may not be His plan for you but, rather, your plan for you. When have you last asked Him what He would like you to do? Perhaps you should do that today.

Pastors often teach their parishioners the notion of "once saved, always saved." In other words, God cannot revoke His salvation promise once someone has accepted Jesus as his or her Savior. What did we just learn about this from the words of Jesus? He said, "If you are lukewarm, I will spit you out of my mouth" and His brother James told us that faith without works is dead. According to the Bible, then, are we "always saved?" For those who are saved and exhibit good works, the truth is that God will not take away your salvation, but I believe you personally can give it away. Pastors may argue that somewhere along the line you will come back to God or that if you leave the faith, it's because you were never saved in the first place. God gave us a free will, though, and we can, though it's ridiculous, give our salvation away. It is true that God will continue to call us, but we don't have to answer.

2Peter 2:19-22 confirms what I've been saying: "A man is a slave to whatever has mastered him. If they have escaped the corruption of the world by knowing our Lord and Savior Jesus Christ and are again entangled in it and overcome, they are worse off at the end then they were at the beginning. It would have been better for them not to have known the way of righteousness than to have known it and then to turn their backs on the sacred commandment that was passed on to them."

I don't think anything could support what I am saying more than the words of the disciple Peter, who knew and walked with Christ. I have personally seen people give away their salvation. One person who is very close to me has not come back to God despite being gravely ill and despite having people witness to him and pray for an awakening of his salvation. I feel, and I'm joined by many others, that this person may spend eternity in hell as punishment for giving away his salvation. Doesn't James suggest the same thing— that salvation can be given away by taking that gift of God too lightly and not thanking Him by doing works in His name? Other verses to consider in this area are Exodus 32:32-33, Psalm 69:27-28 and Revelation 22:19.

James taught me two other very important things during my reading. First, he talks about the plans you and I make from day to day. He says in chapter 4, verse 13: You who say, 'Today or tomorrow we will go to this or that city, spend a year there and carry on business and make money. Why? You do not even know what will happen tomorrow ... you are a mist that appears for a little while and then vanishes. Instead, you ought to say, 'If it is the Lord's will, we will live and do this and that'." What James is saying here is that as we make plans leaving the Lord out, we are putting ourselves in charge of our lives when, in reality, we haven't got a thing to do with what happens tomorrow. I now catch myself leaving the Lord out and try to give God His rightful place in my life.

I also found words in James that many denominational churches have completely ignored. I can only ask: How can that be? In James 5:14, we are told, "Is any one of you sick? He should call the elders of the church to pray over him and <u>anoint him with oil</u> in the name of the Lord. And the prayer offered in faith will make the sick person well; the Lord will raise him up. If he has sinned, he will be forgiven. Therefore, confess your sins to each other and pray for each other so that you may be healed." Anointing a sick person with oil is a clear directive from the brother of Jesus. When James says: ".... the Lord will raise him up," does that mean the person will be healed on earth or does it mean the Lord *may* heal him or her on earth, but He may choose to do that healing in heaven, as all will be healed there. Whatever, why has the anointing with oil not been instituted in many denominational churches? Does your church anoint people who are sick with oil? If not, why not? Stand up for Jesus, and ask the tough questions of your pastor and church hierarchy. Just be sure you can always back up what you're saying in the Word, and to do that, you have to read it and know it.

As you discuss with your pastor or priest the anointing of oil that James teaches, be careful of the false faith healers you may hear about or encounter. When I was young, religious programs filled the television air waves on Sundays. My dad used to love to watch them, and I enjoyed watching them with him. I especially loved Rex Humbard and his wife Maude Aimee and their services from the Cathedral of Tomorrow in Akron, Ohio. Little did I know that would be the beginning of my love of Gospel music.

I also remember a very young pastor by the name of Oral Roberts. He had an 18,000-seat tent ministry that was televised weekly, and faith healings were a major part of that ministry. Numerous people were "miraculously" healed. Crippled people on crutches and in wheelchairs simply walked away after Oral Roberts laid hands on them. People were also supposedly healed of many diseases. It was amazing—and I know God can miraculously heal—but the more I watched the program, the more skeptical I became. I remember telling my dad that I thought those healings just might be fake. My dad never replied to my suspicions.

The time would come that the ministry of Oral Roberts became suspect. Books have been written about this. In his later years, however, Oral Roberts did many good things for the Lord, including the building of the Christian university that bears his name. I cannot fault him for that, and God alone has the answers to my healing issues with Roberts and other faith healers. I'm simply putting up a red flag of warning to those of you who might hang on to any potential false teachers of a healing faith.

Let me make it clear that I know God can and does heal people. Doctors gave my own mother, stricken with lymphoma at 83, two months to live. She lived another 14 years. No one but God can explain that, but no man heals. Only God can do that, and healing isn't coincidental nor is it for the glorification of man but of God. Be alert to those around you whose motives might not be as pure as you think they are. Ask God for discernment.

Only a few more books of the Bible to read and I would encounter the Book of Revelation—the book that cemented my mission to write this book. I'm excited to share that Bible book with you. So, you read on your own the books of I Peter through the book of Jude who, by the way, is said to be, like James, another earthly brother of Jesus. His is the only book in the Bible devoted to apostasy or the story of those who have received light but not life because they know the written Word but not the living Word, exactly what I was guilty of. Are you now thinking that might be you, too?

In the next few chapters, I'll do my best, with the leading of the Holy Spirit, to take you through one of the most exciting books of the Bible—the Book of Revelation. You could never imagine or even fathom what is in store for you in that book. Following that, you'll learn the exciting story of how God used my new Bible knowledge to turn my life and that of my family toward Him in ways we couldn't possibly have imagined—and we've never looked back.

CHAPTER 5

WILL YOU MISS IT?

S oon my year of reading the Bible would be over. I couldn't believe the time had flown so quickly. More importantly, I couldn't believe all of the information I had gained and the excitement that the new awareness brought. I naively believed I would never forget a word of what I read. That's how deeply God's Word had penetrated my heart. It had been an eye-opening, incredible journey, and the end was in sight. The problem was: The end meant tackling the Book of Revelation.

I knew very little about Revelation. I had been told that it was much too hard to understand because it was all written in symbolism. I was familiar, though, with a couple of verses: 1) "Be faithful, even to the point of death, and I will give you the crown of life." (Rev. 2:10) and 2) "I stand at the door and knock. If anyone hears my voice and opens the door, I will come in and eat with him and he with me." (Rev. 3:20). I had also heard about the streets of gold in heaven and had been told that was in Revelation. Other than that, I never heard a pastor or family member speak about the book.

It was tough for me to get excited about reading Revelation, and I almost decided not to. Probably the only reason I read it is because I had made a promise to God that I would read the Bible from cover to cover. So, I decided to get going and skip over all the symbolism, certain I would finish it well ahead of time. I decided that if generations before me, as well as pastors, couldn't figure out Revelation, there was no way I was going to do it. What I learned, though, is that when Satan, the great deceiver, wants his way— whether it is with a pastor, a church hierarchy, or even devoted Christians, he can turn truth into lies in a heartbeat. In this case, he has, for hundreds of years, been in charge of a lie that nearly took me away from the one book of the Bible that changed my life almost more than any other.

Before I share the Book of Revelation with you, I want to be certain you understand some important things. First, do not read this book before reading **all** of the other books of the Bible. It's true that without knowledge of the entire Old and New Testaments, you will be lost in Revelation. What does that tell you about our church hierarchy and pastoral community? They haven't read all of the Bible so they couldn't possibly understand or teach Revelation. Second, do not read it with one ounce of opinion from your church; read it with the Holy Spirit alone. Third, do not believe the lie that it is full of symbolism and you can't possibly understand it. Don't allow Satan to do that kind of number on you. Fourth, be prepared for a life-changing experience.

As you know, with very few exceptions, the world completely missed the first coming of Jesus. They were waiting for the arrival of a king and not a baby born in Bethlehem, even though the prophet Micah told them the details of not only Jesus' birth but who He would be. How could they miss it? They were so blindsided by the Pharisees, Sadducees, rabbis and others that they refused to see their Savior standing directly in front of them. I believe that those who don't read the Book of Revelation or read it with a doctrinal bias will very likely miss the second coming of Jesus, too—or at least have no clue just how close His coming is. I believe the biblical illiteracy of mankind will result in well-deserved consequences. How long has God given everyone to read His Word in its entirety? How long has He given you? It's one book, folks—just *one*. God said, "My people are destroyed for lack of knowledge." There is no one on earth who places the label "Christian" on himself or herself who should speak about his or her faith without knowledge, and that knowledge comes from studying God's Word—including the Book of Revelation. Digesting what the church or the pastor says without investigation is, in my opinion, a wasted life for Jesus Christ—and mine was one of those.

The Book of Revelation is a vision given to the Apostle John while he was exiled by the Roman government on the island of Patmos, off the coast of Asia, about 95 A.D. It is an amazing account of the second coming of Christ and the events leading up to that. Verse 3 of chapter 1 should tell you why this is an important book to read: "Blessed is the one who reads the words of this prophecy and blessed are those who hear it and take to heart what is written in it, because the time is near." Once you have read the Bible, including Revelation, no one will ever be able to convince you that God doesn't have a specific plan for the second coming. God wants you to be a witness to the unfolding of that plan, but how can you witness if you don't know the plan? And how can you know the plan if you don't read and study it?

Before we discuss Revelation, it's important to ask yourself why your church doesn't preach and teach this Bible book. I can tell you with certainty that the Lutheran Church didn't teach it as long as I was a member. What's the reason for that? I've done a little research into that. First and foremost, the seminary doesn't teach this book to pastoral candidates. Lutheran doctrine teaches that this book and its prophecies were fulfilled in 70 A.D. so there's no reason to study it before becoming a pastor. Let's consider the "logic" of that. John wrote Revelation in 95 A.D.—25 years after 70 A.D. Verse 3 says we should read this book "because the time is **near**." He didn't say "the time has passed." Why has no one questioned the churches' 70 A.D. stand? Might it be due to "blind indoctrination" and "biblical illiteracy"?

It is also often said that Revelation is simply an allegorical book. If you and I read the book without doctrinal bias, we will, I promise you, say to ourselves, "That doctrinal position isn't possible in light of Scripture," and we're absolutely right because *all* Scripture is God-breathed and has been placed there for our learning! How then did the Lutheran Church and others get such an unscriptural idea of Revelation? Besides, Jesus Himself said, "Blessed is the one who reads the words of this prophesy and blessed are those who hear it and take to heart what is written." Shame on churches that don't teach Revelation or preach it. That position directly disobeys the words of Jesus.

Dr. Jack Van Impe, who has devoted his life to studying and memorizing the Bible and whose nation-wide television show focuses on events leading to Jesus' second coming, helps us understand how the churches fell away from the Revelation truth. Dr. Van Impe said the following in his magazine *Perhaps Today*: "Gibbons, in his enlightening volume entitled *The Decline and Fall of the Roman Empire,* lists 21 church fathers who for 430 years proclaimed the ... reign of Christ upon planet earth. Some such as St. Iraneous and St. Justine Martyr were so scripturally convinced of the coming Golden Age that they said, 'No one who rejects ... the reign of Christ should even call himself a Christian.'"[2]

What happened to change the churches' stand? Something called "Replacement Theology" invaded it. Unable to read and understand Revelation—probably because of biblical illiteracy— church leaders simply replaced the word "Israel" with the word "church" and the word "Jerusalem" with the word "heaven." That ended the truth of biblical prophesy in many denominational churches. Satan continues to enjoy the neglect of God's Word that has taken over many denominational seminaries, churches, and their people. Amazingly, denominational seminarians graduate knowing they've never read the entire Bible and haven't questioned a thing.

I have read that for Lutherans, Catholics and Presbyterians, this doctrinal difficulty only got worse when St. Augustine attempted to read Revelation. When he couldn't understand it, he simply accepted the teaching of Replacement Theology. If you decide to finally read the entire Bible, including Revelation, with just the help of the Holy Spirit and/or a nondenominational guide, be prepared. Like me, you just might think twice about remaining in the doctrine of your heritage. Are you willing to put God above man in a choice such as that? If so, let's get started, and let's take a look at our future through the eyes of the man to whom God gave the vision—the Apostle John.

The Book of Revelation is so intense and so full of information that I can't possibly go through every verse of it with you. There are many excellent writers who have already done that. My goal is to get you to see the end of the world and the return of Christ—a return that I conclude could happen in my lifetime. I believe I can support that belief through the words of Scripture. To do so, I will have to refer to the Old Testament as well as the New. Because my goal is to have you read it for yourself, I will cover only the basics. I hope I "whet your appetite" enough to get you to want to read more and then challenge your church's stand on its doctrine of Replacement Theology, also called amillennialism.

Since we know that Revelation is about Jesus' second coming, it's also important to know that the book's purpose is to show you what will happen at that time. God wanted the Israelites to be prepared for

Jesus' first coming, but they weren't. Now, He is asking you and me to be prepared for His second coming, but unless we read the entire Bible, as it should be read—without doctrinal bias—we, like the early Jews, may miss the second coming, too. What a tragedy that would be!

CHAPTER 6

CHURCHES JESUS COMES BACK TO

So, what will the world be like when Jesus comes again? Matthew 24 gives us the signs of the end of the world as we know it. Verse 27 takes us all the way back to the beginning of time and God's terrible punishment on mankind during the days of Noah. Jesus says: "But as the days of Noah were, so shall the coming of the Son of Man be. For as in the days that were before the flood, they were eating and drinking, marrying and giving in marriage, until the day that Noah entered into the ark and knew not until the flood came and took them all away; so shall also the coming of the Son of Man be." In other words, Jesus is saying that people were so busy with their lives that they missed God. They were into themselves and not into Him. Despite Noah's best efforts to witness for more than 120 years, people were shocked when the flood waters came and carried them away.

What does the Bible tell us life was like in Noah's day? In other words, what led to the flood? Genesis Chapter 6 tells us that "the sons of God saw that the daughters of men were beautiful and they married any of them they chose." In other words, they left God out of the decision as to whom they should marry and, thus, married heathen women. "The Lord saw how great man's wickedness on the earth had become and that every inclination of the thoughts of his heart was filled with pain... Now the earth was corrupt in God's sight and was full of violence." Noah was the only righteous man on earth. That is the scene Jesus portrays for us as to the status of our world when He returns.

Not long after Noah, the cities of Sodom and Gomorrah became a problem for God. The Bible says that "men from every part of the city of Sodom—both young and old—surrounded the house. They called to Lot, 'Where are the men who came to you tonight. Bring them out to us so that we can have sex with them.' The angel of the Lord said to Lot, 'The outcry of the Lord against its people is so great that He has sent us to destroy it'." Ruth Bell Graham, wife of television evangelist Billy Graham, wrote in regards to these two cities: "If America does not repent and God does nothing, then He must apologize to Sodom and Gomorrah." Mrs. Graham saw an America that she and I both believe God will judge and judge soon. Neither she nor I see an America that is repenting. Rather, we both see an America that is turning more and more away from God, believing it is too big and too important to fail. What America doesn't realize is that it is not in charge. God is. One day, all of mankind will see that.

People want to see God only as "love." It is true that God is love, but He also says, "Whom I loveth, I chastiseth." Soon, He will chastise the entire world for the sins that we see every day all around us, and the plan for that judgment can be found in the book of Revelation. Keep in mind that the Bible says no man knows the day or the hour that these things will occur—only the Father knows. The Bible also says, though, that we can know the season. You won't recognize the season, however, if you don't read the Word. Many will be deceived. I pray that after reading this chapter and those remaining in Part II, you won't be one of the deceived.

The Book of Revelation takes us from the establishment of the church to the end of the world as we know it. God wrote it so we who read it will know His plan and not be afraid as we see events unfolding. God did not make Revelation difficult unless you choose not to read the entire Bible first, and He expected all of us to make that a priority in our lifetime. I have no doubt about that. Why would He write a book for the purpose of having only the learned men of the church able to read it? He wrote the book for *all* to read and understand. The question I ask is: Why aren't people reading it? The answer: Deception created by some churches to which generations of Christians have belonged—the idea from the church that those in leadership know more than mankind ever could. I learned by reading the Bible what a manipulation by Satan that is!

Chapters 1-4 of Revelation are about seven churches. Why only seven? Because seven has always been associated with perfection where God is concerned. In Rev. 1:18-19, John hears these words: "I am the Living One; I was dead, and behold I am alive for ever and ever! ... Write, therefore, what you have seen, what is now and what will take place later." John wrote Revelation because God told him to. Chapter 1 is "what you have seen." Chapters 2 and 3 are "what is." Chapters 4-22 include "what will take place later." John writes Revelation for us under the direction of God.

In Chapter 2, God begins his warning to seven earthly operating churches. These aren't fairytale churches but actual churches that existed at the time. As you read about them, I have a feeling you will see your church in one or more of them. That's the idea. That's why God took the time to discuss them. He wants us to examine the churches we attend in light of those He shares with us in Revelation. If you find your church in these seven, perhaps you should consider changing churches. Also, keep in mind that Paul tells us we personally are the church of God since the Holy Spirit resides in us. Our "bodies are the temple of the Holy Spirit." How is your own bodily church doing in light of these Revelation churches?

The first church of Revelation is the church in Ephesus. Ephesus was a very important part of the Roman Empire. Paul's letter to the Ephesians is the church spoken about in Revelation. God first shows the church ways in which it persevered. Yet in verse 4, He says, "You have forsaken your first love." They were, like many of us, probably worshipping rotely and routinely and not reaching beyond their doors to the lost. Why did this happen? They lost their zeal for God. How about you? Do you go to church on Sunday and simply go through the motions? Do you know the service so well that, without realizing it, you aren't really worshipping God but simply doing what you have always done? Have you, then, also forgotten your first love? Or, in reality, is your denominational church really your first love? Have you placed the love of your church above your love for God? What message is your church sending to others? Is it biblically based and Christ centered?

If we are in tune with God and make Him first in our lives, He may call us away from our churches for all the right reasons. Sometimes, though, we are so heritage-minded and/or tradition-minded that we wouldn't leave a church even if it is God who calls us away. In fact, we're often so blinded by our allegiance to a denomination that absolutely nothing would take us away. Is it more important, though, to attach ourselves blindly to our denomination, or should we attach ourselves to God and to Him alone?

The second church of Revelation is the church of Smyrna. The congregation suffered terrible persecution at the hands of what God calls "a synagogue of Satan." God warns this church that they will suffer, but they are not to be afraid. The suffering will not go on forever, God reminds them. As my mother used to say, "This, too, shall pass." That is what God is telling the Smyrna church. The message to us in this story is that God is always with us and will see us through even the most difficult situations. He also shares in our suffering. In Acts 9:5, Saul (now Paul) is on the road to Damascus when he heard a voice and said, "Who are you, Lord?" The answer: "I am Jesus whom you are persecuting." Paul must have said to himself, "When did I persecute you?" What Paul didn't realize is that when God's people are persecuted for His sake, He is persecuted, too, because He lives inside of us.

God said to the people of the Smyrna church: "Do not be afraid of what you are about to suffer ... you will be persecuted for ten days." Many Bible scholars believe this church was one that was fed to the lions in Rome. How horrible would that be! Next, though, is the very well-known verse the people must have clung to: "Be faithful, even to the point of death, and I will give you a crown of life." These Christians had been given a word of comfort from God—a personal note—and went to the mouths of the lions with courage.

I have asked myself many times if I really have the courage necessary to die for my faith as these people did. The answer is, of course, I must. Should that occur, the Bible tells us not to be afraid. Jesus said in Matthew that at the end of the world, Christians will be persecuted as they are now in many parts of the world. Religious persecution occurs even in America, sometimes in our court system where we Christians seek justice. Have you ever said the word "God" in public? Heaven forbid! People either back away as if you have a contagious disease (and wouldn't it be wonderful if they caught it?) or they are angrily confrontational. Are there signs that religious persecution will get worse. I believe there are signs of that everywhere. The truth, though, is that Jesus is right there with us and is being persecuted as well. God will prevail in the end. In the words of the old hymn that still ring true: "Trust and obey for there's no other way to be happy in Jesus but to trust and obey." If I trust and obey, God has promised He will be with me even in the midst of persecution and will one day give me a crown of life.

The third church of Revelation is the church of Pergamum. Four cults occupied this city, and its church was trying to balance the "one foot in the world and one foot in the church" philosophy. Though the church remained faithful to God under the worst of circumstances, some in the church were tolerant of sin. It's the "let's be nice" phenomena, or "they can't help it". Does this sound like any church in America? How about those churches that accept such biblical sins as homosexuality? If God calls it sin, it's sin—period. Man cannot derail God for the sake of tolerance. Yet, that happens every Sunday in churches across America and the world. Are there consequences for looking the other way at sin? In the church of Pergamum, that answer came when the angel said to this church, "I know where you live—where Satan has his throne." Does Satan have his throne in your church?

On the outside, the church of Pergamum looked perfect, but some within it were more tolerant than faithful. Paul said in I Corinthians 10:21: "You cannot drink the cup of the Lord and the cup of demons, too." Hebrews 12:14 says, "Without holiness, no one will see the Lord." Standing firm for God means standing firmly against sin. There is no in between. This church clearly missed that point, as well as the "go and sin no more" words that Jesus Himself taught. Are you attending a church that openly accepts sin as okay? If so, perhaps it is time to move on.

Yes, churches of Satan, though with a Christian exterior and name, exist today. Use the Word of God to stand up against such churches. "Do not merely listen to the word and so deceive yourselves. Do what it says." (James 1:22) Hebrews 4:12 says: "For the *Word of God (the Bible) is living and active*, sharper than any double-edged sword. It penetrates even to dividing soul and spirit, joints and marrow; it judges the thoughts and attitudes of the heart." Know the Bible so you can share it with others, and know what your church stands for. Don't get caught on judgment day with one foot in the world, trying to make excuses for yourself.

The fourth church is the church of Thyatira. This church was located in a community of ordinary working-class people. It was the place where Lydia of the Bible, a dealer in purple cloth, lived and where Paul's message led to faith and baptism of her and her household. This was a church of good deeds and love. It had grown beyond a church that simply worshipped the Lord one day a week. It became an olive tree that blossomed for Jesus.

The church, however, had a flaw. It allowed a prophetess to lead members of the church into sexual immorality and the sacrificing of food to idols. How did she accomplish this in the midst of a Godly congregation? She undoubtedly was very charismatic and may have even been an amazing speaker who enveloped her audience. She was obviously what I would call "slick and shiny." People were drawn to her. Do you know anyone like this? Are you easily led by someone with a "slick and shiny" message? Do you have difficulty "seeing the forest for the trees?" Ask God for discernment. In this day and age, we need people of discernment to say the right things and do the right things for God. Many well-meaning people have been led astray by something that sounds so good.

God tells us that He tried to get the prophetess to repent but she would not. So, He said: "I will cast her on a bed of suffering and I will make those who commit adultery with her suffer intensely. Then all the churches will know that I am he who searches the hearts and minds and *I will repay each of you according to your deeds*." God obviously is not the nice guy who sits back and says, "Oh well, things happen down there." He's tough but forgiving as long as we repent and work at sinning no more. It should be clear, though, that God doesn't simply "look the other way," and heaven isn't a free pass. It is up to each of us to search our hearts and our churches and remove evil from them or stay away from those we believe might have evil intentions. "Put on the full armor of God so that you can take your stand against the devil's schemes." (Ephesians 6:11)

The fifth church is the dead church of Sardis, which was a city rich in money but its church was poor in spirit. The church had fallen away from the basis of the Christian faith—Jesus. God tells this church that they are dead. The church looked good on the outside but was sinful on the inside. Some churches today are dead even though they are a pillar of the community and have an active membership. The people in these churches have not grown beyond a basic faith and many have slipped away into sin. People who possess a basic faith go to church every week because that is what they were taught to do. They never go beyond that stage. They go through the motions while they're in attendance, often fully believing they have worshipped the Lord. But, they have not. They have only attended church. Some people are in attendance to improve their social status or their businesses. For some, then, the church is nothing more than a social club—a community center. Even many denominational churches—their pastors and hierarchy—just go through the motions each and every week. It is simply the ritual of the church that reigns every Sunday rather than the relationship with Christ that He demands. Doing your duty isn't pleasing to the Lord. "Using" the Lord for personal gain isn't acceptable in His eyes either.

How can a church really be an alive and witnessing church if its members accept sin as normal even though such sin is an abomination to God? How can any church be alive if its pastor hasn't read the Bible from cover to cover? Has your church honored Jesus by knowing the entire Word, or have you simply slipped by using a doctrinal book rather than the entire Bible? Has your church accepted unrepented sin as the norm? Is there real enthusiasm for Jesus in your church? Are you willing to evangelize for Him and are you tithing? Is your pastor or priest encouraging you to do just that? Finally, are you being taught messages about the End Times? If not, why aren't you looking for another church?

I believe a pastor or priest should be required to read the Bible entirely every five years. I don't think that's too much to ask. The deacons or elders should then test the pastor. Guess what? To do that, the deacons and elders would have to read the whole Bible, too. Isn't that a unique and wonderful idea? In many states, school teachers have to take classes every few years to update and reinforce their skills. Shouldn't the pastor in your church also be required to know the book he teaches—the Bible? After all, it's only *one* book. In light of the questions I've just asked you—think about it, now—is your church alive or dead? How do you think God would rate your church and/or your pastor or priest?

The sixth church of Revelation is the good works church of Philadelphia. God tells this church that "since you have kept my command to endure patiently, I will also keep you from the hour of trial that is going to come upon the whole world to test those who live on the earth." This is the church to which all of us should want to belong. This church is faithful, and God rewards that faithfulness with the promise we all want to hear—that He will keep them "from the hour of trial that is going to come upon the whole world." It's the "trial" described in Revelation. What does "faithful" really mean? Does it mean an attachment to doctrine rather than the Word? Is it a church that witnesses or waits? Is it a church that looks the other way at sin? Is it known for its "socialness" or its faithfulness? Is it a church that prepares its people for the return of Christ and makes them aware of the signs of the End Times? How does your church compare to the faithful church of Philadelphia? Ask yourself: Will your church be spared from the "hour of trial" or will God say: "You still have something to learn down there"?

The seventh and final church of Revelation is the lukewarm church of Laodicea. Laodicea was a very wealthy city. Yet, that wealth and prosperity may have been their downfall. God said: "I know your deeds, that you are neither hot nor cold. Because you are lukewarm ... I am about to spit you out of my mouth. You say, 'I am rich; I have acquired wealth and do not need a thing'. But you do not realize that you are wretched, pitiful, poor, blind and naked." What is God telling us here? The Bible says money is *a root of all evil*. Wealth, success, and prosperity can lead man to believe he has no need for God because he is his own god. He may conclude that those who have a need for God are weak because people like him are strong. What does God say, though? He tells those who believe their success comes from them that they are "wretched, pitiful, poor, blind and naked." Money can and often does blind man's eyes to the reality of eternity.

The world has to one day realize that money doesn't mean a thing. It is fleeting, and so are we. What this verse says is that if you don't have Jesus, you are "wretched, pitiful, poor, blind and naked." Can't you see a lukewarm—or even worse—philosophy in our world today? People often behave in a manner toward God that wasn't evident even 50 years ago. They don't feel they need God because they have money—lots of it. Interestingly, though, in a flash, riches can be taken away by God. That has happened recently in America, hasn't it? Greedy men have stolen hoards of money from unsuspecting, trusting Americans. Lifetime savings are gone. What is God saying to America?

People who have earthly goods often believe that they alone earned those. It was *their* hard work, *their* stamina, and *their* intelligence that got them where they are so they don't need to go to church or serve the Lord. In verse 19 of chapter 3, though, God says: "Those I love I rebuke and discipline. So be earnest and repent." God demands first place in your life and mine. "You shall have no other gods before Me." He says that he is a jealous God. An emphasis on *you* apart from God makes you a "god" in your own life. Jesus tells us in Matthew 6:19-21: "Do not store up for yourselves treasures on earth, where moth and rust destroy, and where thieves break in and steal. But store up for yourselves treasures in heaven ... For where your treasure is, there your heart will also be."

Those of us who succeed in life have God to thank for that and not ourselves. God promises to discipline any who fail to see that. It is fine to be rich as long as you recognize where that wealth comes from and as long as you use it to further God's kingdom. Rich or poor, God's people are to be busy reaching the lost for Jesus Christ and growing their own faith. Just attending church isn't enough. That is a lukewarm Christian. Is that you? If so, God says He will spit you out of His mouth—no matter how many Sundays you've been in church. Church isn't a house of duty or a community center open each week for social gatherings. Church is a place where God is to be intently worshipped; and when its doors open at the end of the service, that is when *your* service in His name is to begin and is to continue until you worship Him again the following week. Do you have a need to repent for your lackadaisical worship and/or your week-long vacations from God? Repent now. Be on fire for the Lord and do His will. That is how He expects all of us to live.

As I think about this final church, I can't help but remember the beautiful churches I visited in Europe—too numerous to count and now virtually empty. Their spires seem to touch the sky, and the pure gold and other jewels found inside of them are astounding. Surrounding those incredibly beautiful churches, though, are communities that are both spiritually blind and biblically illiterate. They have lost touch with God. Think about this: Is God really interested in a beautiful earthly church, or is He interested in the beautiful, faithful souls that no longer worship there? How did the European churches die? By now, you should know the answer to that. Can that "death" happen to America? Is the answer "can it" or "has it" or "how soon will it"?

We have just discussed seven churches in Revelation. Are those in the Bible for us to ignore as simply churches from the past? There is no evidence of that. The seven churches we have just read about clearly exist in society today. Yours might be one of them. Take a good look at your church, and ask God to show you where, in His eyes, your church stands. My life completely changed when I did that.

Is the book of Revelation allegorical? Is it a book whose work was finished in 70 A.D. as many denominational churches believe? Absolutely not, and reading this book is the first step in understanding that. Take a second look, denominational churches. Take a second look, Christians. God left one book—the Bible—for you to read! What's your excuse for not doing so?

CHAPTER 7

WHAT'S YET TO COME

As I took my final steps toward the completion of reading the entire Bible, little did I know that God was about to cement a change in my life and my husband's life forever. It would all be so amazing, so mind-boggling. There is so much power in the Word giving so much knowledge. I'm so blessed to have read it and to have met personally a God I never knew before.

My shock as I began Chapter 4 of Revelation is that I only got to verse 6 when I recognized that I had read the exact same thing in Ezekiel 1:4, Isaiah 6 and Daniel 7. I sat in amazement. John knew the Old Testament, so the vision he received at this point must have stunned him, as it did me. This is one of many reasons why you must read the Old Testament before the New Testament and certainly before you read Revelation. Let's begin in verse 1 of that chapter first, though, as I found that eye-opening, too.

I had always been taught that when Jesus comes back, a trumpet will sound. That was confirmed for me in II Thessalonians 4:16. Some believe that the trumpeter will be the angel Gabriel. Since my brother was a wonderfully talented trumpet player, I knew I was one who wouldn't miss the second coming call, and neither would my sister. You see, our brother was not only a great trumpet player, but he also loved to aggravate. Since he was the oldest and I, the mistake, was the youngest, his target was always my sister who was just three years younger than he was. Can you imagine a great trumpet player blowing directly into your ear? Good thing my sister loved him. He and his son went to heaven in 1959, and today, we all—even my sister—miss that often annoying trumpet call.

When I got to Revelation 4:1, I began to think quite differently about the final call. This is what I read: "The first *voice* which I heard was as it were of a trumpet *talking* with me." In reality, this wasn't an actual trumpet but a voice that sounded like a trumpet. Will there really be a trumpet call? Maybe not. I honestly wonder now if the "trumpet call" announcing Jesus' second coming will actually be the voice of Jesus Himself. Perhaps that is why He said while on earth: "My sheep hear my voice and they know me." Imagine the sweet but resounding trumpet voice of Jesus in your ear announcing His earthly return. That will be the moment of all moments.

Chapter 6 of Revelation begins the terrible "Great Tribulation" hour on the earth—the one Jesus Himself spoke of. Before we discuss that, you need to understand a word you may not have heard before. The word is "rapture." The majority of people who have read and studied the Bible and who, like me, believe in a literal translation of Revelation (just as we believe in a literal translation of the rest of the Bible because God Himself said that He wrote it: "<u>All</u> Scripture is God-breathed") feel the rapture will take place before the Tribulation. What does the word rapture mean? It means "a snatching away." I Thessalonians 4:16-17 says: "For the Lord Himself shall descend from heaven with a shout, with the voice of the archangel and with the trump of God and the dead in Christ shall rise first. <u>Then we who are still alive and remain</u> shall be caught up together with them in the clouds to meet the Lord in the air and so shall we ever be with the Lord." I Corinthians 15:51 says: "Behold, I show you a mystery (notice Paul uses the word "mystery"). <u>We shall not all sleep</u> but we shall all be changed, in a moment, in the twinkling of an eye, at the last trump." Notice, Paul says that not everyone born to earth will die physically. Some will simply be "snatched away" or raptured.

One day, we will hear the voice of the Lord, and we'll be gone to be with the Lord and all those who died and were saved. While we will be "snatched away" from earth, the dead in Christ shall be "snatched away" from their graves. Amazingly, this rapture will take place in eleven one-hundredths of a second, according to Dr. Jack Van Impe's *Prophesy Bible*. That is how long the "twinkling of an eye" is. In less than a second, I will be reunited with my parents, brother and nephew, brother-in-law, grandparents, extended family, friends and more. I can't wait!

People might say, "Well, so what? We have all heard that Jesus is coming again and He will take us to heaven." That's true; but when you put this together with the rest of the story—if you're open to it—you will see that this is actually the rapture or "snatching away" of the church All those who truly believe that Jesus died on the cross so we might be saved—and if they have served God, not for salvation but out of great love for that salvation—will be part of the rapture, God's "snatching away" of His people. He will snatch us away but, according to the Bible, will bring us back when He returns to judge the earth one final time.

People on earth will wonder what happened to those who suddenly disappeared from the earth, won't they? That is why it is important to witness—not just about death or the rapture but so those who are left behind will know why we're gone and will repent, even during the torment of the Tribulation. They'll say, "(<u>Put your name here</u>) said this would happen. There must be a God whom I have to believe in for salvation." Remember, folks: The only thing you can take to heaven is another person.

Coming one day soon is a seven-year period of history that ends in the greatest battle ever fought on the earth, The Battle of Armageddon. God will be victorious in that battle of all battles and will reign for ever and ever. Before that happens, though, there are many signs, wonders, and actual events that man will encounter, warning him of the coming of the Lord. Information about all of this can be found throughout the Bible—Daniel 7-12, Ezekiel 33-48, Zechariah, Matthew 24, Mark 13, Luke 17 and 21 and the entire book of Revelation. You will be amazed at the identical information offered in all of these biblical books.

The Bible says that the end of life on earth as we know it begins when a peace treaty is signed with Israel. Be alert for the signing of that treaty. Once the peace treaty is signed, there will be an absolute and glorious peace in Israel for a period of three and a half years. People who do not know the Bible will undoubtedly become complacent. Life will seem normal—even glorious. At the end of this time of peace, however, the Great Tribulation will begin and will be the earthly horror of all horrors—much like the flood of Noah's day. Though that resulted in a quick death, this will be long and painful.

At the end of three and a half years of peace, seven seals will be poured out from heaven over the entire earth. These seals are exactly like the plagues that God inflicted on Pharaoh and his people in Egypt when Pharaoh wouldn't allow God's people—the Israelites—to leave. Were the Egyptian plagues a foreshadowing—a teaching—for those of us who came later to learn from and be aware of? I believe they are. Let's examine all seven of the seals and see.

The first seal is in chapter 6, verse 2 of Revelation. There is a white horse with a rider carrying a bow. He received a crown and went forth conquering the earth. This is a man called the Antichrist, whom we will discuss in detail later. Suffice it to say that this man is the one who will sign the peace treaty with Israel but later controls the whole world, calls himself God, and seats himself in the temple of God in Jerusalem (II Thessalonians 2:3-4). You may say, "That can't happen because there is no temple in Jerusalem—nothing but steps and a Wailing Wall." The truth is, there isn't a temple *yet.* According to Rabbi Chaim Richman of the Temple Institute and a member of the Israeli Sanhedrin, "The third temple is ready for building. All furnishings are in storage, priests are already trained, and the temple is prefabricated off-site."[3] This fulfills the prophecy of Daniel 9:24-25.

The second seal is a man on a red horse. According to Rev. 6:4, power was given to this rider to take peace from the earth. How is peace taken from the earth? "Wars and rumors of wars"—those that Jesus promised would come. What is the significance of the color red here? For the answer to this, we must read Ezekiel 38. The words in verse 3—Gog, Magog, Meshech and Tubal (some say cities in Russia)—say, (I will) "bring you out with your whole army. Persia (present day Iran), Cush (parts of Africa) and Put (Egypt) will be with them....also Gomer and Beth Togarmah from the far north with all its troops—the many nations with you.....You will invade a land that has recovered from war, whose people were gathered from many nations to the mountains of Israel....they had been brought out from the nations and now all of them live in safety. You will advance against my people Israel... When Gog attacks the land of Israel, my anger will be aroused, declares the Sovereign Lord."

God is saying that countries will, at the End Times, invade Israel. Many believe Red Russia is the "red horse" spoken of in Revelation 6. Today, do you see any possibility that Russia might invade Israel? Have you been listening to the news or reading a newspaper lately? Iran's leader, Ahmadinejad, has stated that he wants to "wipe Israel off the map." Who might his ally be in such an effort? None other than Russia. Vladimir Putin, once seemingly a friend of former President Bush, now appears to be America's enemy and, thus, Israel's enemy as well.

It is interesting to note that Revelation discusses the fact that people will be gathered from many nations to the mountains of Israel. Since 1948 when Israel became a nation, that has been happening. When John wrote Revelation, what was his scope of knowledge in regards to the word "many nations"? An Israelite, he was exiled to the island of Patmos where he received the "revelation." Did he know much, if anything, about Europe, Asia, the United States, South America, etc.? I doubt that he did, but he dutifully used the words given to him by God—"many nations"—so those who are now living would see God's plan written thousands of years ago being fulfilled. Amazing!

The third seal is a black horse with a rider and a balance in his hand. Bible scholars believe this seal represents the famine and inflation that usually follows war. Ezekiel 7 says: "Inside are plague and famine; those in the country will die by the sword and those in the city will be devoured by famine and plague ... they will throw silver into the streets and their gold will be an unclean thing. Their silver and gold will not be able to save them in the day of the Lord's wrath." All the money in the world isn't going to save the world from the horrors of the Tribulation.

The fourth seal is a rider on a pale horse. He was given the authority to kill with swords and with hunger and with disease. This rider was called Death and Hell. One fourth of the earth's population is killed by this rider. People, if you believe in God, you have to realize that He won't be tested forever, nor will He be mocked. People want desperately to believe that God is love, and He is; but, he is also judge and disciplinarian. If you have read any of the Old Testament, you quickly realize that God is anything but the "always good guy." Man is not supposed to believe what makes him feel "comfy cozy." Man is held to the words of Scripture, and the Bible doesn't always show a God who simply loves and looks the other way. God loves the nation of Israel—His chosen people—but look what He has allowed the people of that nation to go through. The end result of every difficulty the Israelis have faced, though, is victory.

The fifth seal displayed "the souls of those who had been slain because of the Word of God and the testimony they had maintained." These were the people who accepted Christ during the Tribulation. God does not want anyone lost; but the requirement for eternity with God is believing that Jesus died on the cross for our sins and thanking Him for that gift by growing a fig tree in our lives that blossoms with works of thanks. If people believe in Jesus during the Tribulation, they will be saved—I didn't say that; God said it in Revelation—and the cries discussed in verse 10 are those people for whom the Tribulation events allowed them to believe. I know there are denominationalists who will not believe that God will save those who did not originally believe. It's time to believe it, though, since God said it. Read Rev. 7:9-10, 13-14.

This is, again, one of many reasons that we have to witness. Those who believe before the Tribulation will be raptured, and you want that for the people you care about. You don't want those you love to have to go through the Tribulation horrors. If your witness doesn't seem to reach people now, though, it may do so during the Tribulation. You will have told them where you are. You will have foretold the future, and they will remember. So, with whom will you leave this salvation message?

During the sixth seal, there is an earthquake. The sun becomes black, and the moon becomes blood. Stars fall from the sky, and every mountain and island is moved from the places where they have been. The Bible says that the mighty men of earth—kings, princes, generals, the rich, etc.,—hide themselves in mountain caves and rocks (as if God, who is omni-present, can't find them). How do we know this isn't simply symbolic? Jesus said in Matthew 24:29 as He quotes Isaiah 13:10 and 34:4: "The sun will be dark-ened and the moon will not give its light; the stars will fall from the sky, and the heavenly bodies will be shaken." What Jesus said in Matthew and what Isaiah prophesied many years before Him actually occurs in Revelation 6. If, as we believe, God created the earth, He certainly knows exactly how to destroy it.

With the unveiling of the seventh seal, God's final punishment for wicked men is fulfilled—the punish-ment He has long promised. In chapter 8, verse 1 of Revelation, we understand the horror of this final seal as we read that there is silence in heaven for a half hour prior to it. An angel then takes fire from the altar of God and casts it down to the earth and the trumpets sound. The first trumpet rains hail and fire mingled with blood to the earth. This fire burns 1/3 of all the earth's trees and every blade of green grass. The second trumpet sounds, a burning mountain is cast into the sea, and the sea becomes blood. One-third of the creatures of the sea die, and one-third of the ships are lost. The third trumpet sounds. A giant star falls from heaven upon the rivers. The waters become poisoned.

At the sound of the fourth trumpet, one third of the sun, moon, and stars will be darkened. The fifth trumpet gives the command that a star will fall from heaven to earth, and the devil will receive the keys to the bottomless pit. The bottomless pit will be opened, and smoke will come up like that of a huge furnace. Locusts will come upon the earth. They are given commands by God not to hurt the grass of the earth, nor any green thing nor any tree but only those men who do not have the seal of God on their foreheads. (If you've read chapter 7, you will see that multitudes of men were sealed for God by 144,000 Jewish witnesses from every tribe of Israel.) Those without the seal will not be killed but will be tortured for five months. The Bible tells us that the men who had not accepted God's free gift of salvation want to die but will not be allowed to.

With the sixth trumpet, God frees four of Satan's angels who had been bound in the Euphrates River. The four angels kill one third of mankind. In verse 16 of chapter 9, we see that a battle is about to take place with an army of 200 million soldiers. How can mankind gather this incredible number of soldiers? If you have watched the news in recent years, you have seen the large size of China's army. China has long insisted on couples having just one child—hopefully a boy—and today China has more than 1.3 billion people. I believe they could come up with 200 million soldiers in no time. How long ago could this have been possible? Not very long. 70 A.D.? I don't think so. In this battle, one-third of men will be killed by fire, smoke, and brimstone. Amazingly, the ones who are left will still refuse to repent; they still worship idols.

With the seventh trumpet, heaven realizes that God's victory over sinful man is fulfilled. Why is this so apparent? God sent two witnesses to earth to prophesy the message of doom for 1,260 days. Despite all that man has done, God still wants people to turn from their wicked ways and accept eternal life through Christ. God will protect these two witnesses until the end of those 1,260 days or 42 months. Satan's buddy, the beast, will then kill the witnesses and leave their bodies in the street for three and one-half days. The Bible says in Rev. 11:9, "The people and kindreds and tongues and nations shall see their dead bodies three days and shall not suffer their dead bodies to be put in the graves." If all of this happened in 70 A.D. as many denominational churches teach, how would a viewing by *every* "people and kindreds and tongues and nations" be possible? It wasn't possible. This viewing has only been possible in very recent years since satellites have allowed man's eyes to be everywhere at once on television sets while seated in their homes. Revelation wasn't written for 70 A.D., folks, but for today.

The people on earth will then rejoice and party, knowing the two witnesses are dead. Then, God will do an amazing thing that He allows the entire world to see. He will grant these two life again, and they will ascend into heaven, just as Jesus did before them. God is the God of life. Mankind will pay for lives taken through abortion, murder, etc. Life and death belong to God, not man. As the two witnesses ascend, an earthquake will come down, and 7,000 people will die.

At this point, you may be thinking, "This is ridiculous. None of this will happen. This is science fiction folklore." I understand how you feel about that. Biblical illiteracy and blind indoctrination in your denominational church has held you prisoner for years and puts doubt in your mind, exactly what Satan hopes. We can't imagine God doing all that has just been written. Many of you are only hearing this for the first time. Such a horrific scene is simply inconceivable. You have to go back to the book of Genesis, however. God gave the people of Noah's day 120 years to repent. Noah built an ark for all those years and told the people why the ark was being built, but people laughed at him, I'm sure. Can you imagine going downtown in the city in which you live, watching someone build a boat for your entire lifetime, and continually listening to him say that God will send a flood to wipe out all who do not believe? Would you believe this old man and his wild stories? We know the people of Noah's day didn't listen because they all died. What do you think happened, though, when the rain came and never stopped and the unbelievers were drowning? Sadly, Noah must have said to himself, "God gave them 120 years. They did this to themselves." Is God giving you this information for you to mock, or is He perhaps giving you a second chance? Think about it.

The seals and trumpets will occur just before Jesus returns, but the information found in the chapters of Revelation beginning with chapter 13 may very well be visible right now to those whose eyes and hearts are open to see. That is the greatest gift God gave me in reading the entire Bible—the ability to read things in the newspaper or see things on television that stir me to wonder just how long it will be before Jesus comes. I truly believe that the election of Barack Obama as president is, to those aware, a sign of the end of mankind as we know it. The next chapter will explain how I see Obama's election fitting into God's plan.

CHAPTER 8

THE BEGINNING
OF THE END?

In Chapter 13 of Revelation, we meet two beasts—the man called the Antichrist and the other, the false prophet. Both are directed by Satan in his final attempt to control the world; but the world, for the most part, won't recognize Satan in action. God is giving people who read and study His Word the opportunity to be aware of and recognize the arrival of these two men. That's why God said reading Revelation will be a blessing.

Do you remember the words of Daniel? The Antichrist will bring peace to Israel—a peace its people have longed for. The world will see this man as remarkable. After all, how many people have tried and failed to bring Israel peace? This man will be a hero. He will undoubtedly be charismatic, communicative, and caring. However, he will also be conniving and cunning. Few will recognize that, though. He is Satan incarnate. When peace eventually comes to

Israel, be aware of the man who actually arranges that peace. Some feel the Antichrist will come from the Old Roman Empire—now the European Union. Others say he will come from Egypt. Wherever he comes from, those who understand God's plan will know him when he comes because of the peace he brings to Israel for a period of three and one-half years. How is it that the world will be taken in by him? It will happen the same way the United States was taken in by Barack Hussein Obama. Democrats, especially, please be open and willing to at least consider this.

Let's analyze the American election of 2008. Tell me what you know about this man named Obama, our president. From ages 6-10, he lived in Indonesia. What do any of us know about his life during those years in a Muslim country? Nothing. He didn't tell us about those years, did he? Neither did anyone else. Why didn't we insist on that knowledge? Because Obama's charisma captivated people beyond reason, as he knew it would. What do you remember about his days at Columbia University other than he dabbled in drugs and met Bill Ayers? Was he a good student? Oops, Columbia didn't release his records (I read they were sealed), and we didn't insist on that important information. What did he see in Ayers? Did he overlook a terrorist? More importantly, as Americans, why did we?

Why did Obama move to Chicago? Might it be that he saw power there? Is there a reason he moved to the area of Chicago he did? Is there a reason he attended a church with 8,000 people, including influential people like Oprah Winfrey? Do we honestly believe he sat in that church for 20 years and didn't know the real Rev. Jeremiah Wright—the man who, in pastoral array, used the name of God in vain to damn America? If Obama did sit there for 20 years and didn't know the real Jeremiah Wright, how is that possible unless Obama doesn't have an ounce of discernment. If that's true, how could America have elected such a man President?

The truth is Americans overlooked things in the 2008 election because Obama was so good at drawing people to him that he didn't have to reveal anything to us or explain anything to us. He simply captivated people, and he still does.

Obama spent only 143 days in the Senate. The rest of the time he planned and campaigned for president. Did those 143 days as a Senator qualify him to be President of the United States? Definitely not, but it gave him a chance to vote "present" enough times so he couldn't be scrutinized when he ran for the office. Few Americans questioned that. People simply questioned Sarah Palin who had been mayor of a city and was a sitting governor of a state. How did that happen? Obama could have told people just about anything, and they would have believed it—and he knew that. The problem is, he is now our president, and we don't know a thing about him—exactly as he had it planned. People allowed him to capture their hearts and their minds. Christians, we are the ones who will be held accountable for that. Obama openly supports all the things that are detestable to God—abortion (including partial birth abortion), stem cell research on aborted fetuses, homosexuality, etc. If you call yourself a Christian and you voted for Obama, who stands against everything God abhors, how will you one day explain that vote to God? You will have to do that, you know. I firmly believe that a Christian vote for Obama was a vote against God. I believe God thinks that, too. God supplied us with a Christian candidate in Sarah Palin, and we voted for the one who loves the world. What is it about the rise of Antichrist that you now don't understand?

Hitler fooled the world, too, and he did it at a time of terrible economic problems in Germany. Sound familiar? The Germans were only too eager to blame their troubles on the Jews who were hard workers and successful. Hitler knew that and used it success- fully to try to achieve his goal of a superior race. He reached the hearts and minds of Germans through their pocketbooks rather than their intellect. They traded the lives of six million Jews via the Holocaust for the economic security and prosperity that Hitler promised. How could they possibly have allowed that to happen? They were "suckered in." Charismatic personalities can do that. They tell you what they know you want to hear.

Good comes out of the hearts of people when they have a head that can see possible danger before them. During the 2008 election, I believe that Americans traded their morals, values, honor, and faith for an untested and untried man who promised the world to the economic downtrodden without revealing one iota more than he cared to about who he really is. I want to make something very clear at this point. I do not pres- ently believe Obama is the Antichrist of Revelation, but if, during his tenure as president, he makes a peace pact with Israel, I will be alert. You see, the Antichrist is going to fool the whole world with his charisma and his ability to bring people together—people who couldn't work out a peace agreement before. The Antichrist will amaze people—just like the election of Obama amazed and frustrated me.

You have seen what charisma without revelation has achieved. Has God allowed that experience in our lives? I know He has. Might that be a punishment to America for our not reading and not living by the Bible? I think that's possible. Will you now miss the Antichrist when he comes on the scene, or will you be more open to someone who seems so right and, in the case of the Antichrist, is so evil? Biblically illiterate people may very well miss the signs that will end the world. All I can say is you had the Bible available to you for a lifetime. It contains all the information you will ever need to know about the future. Whose fault is it that you didn't read it and you don't know the truth?

I pray that Barack Obama is the best president America has ever had. That would be wonderful for all of us. The one thing I know for sure, though, is that God is in charge of all things, so either God chose Obama for us or He allowed him to be our president. We do nothing without God's leadership. We only think we do. My prayer for President Obama is that he becomes a person I someday know something about and is someone who stands up for Godly principles at all times. I don't see that now, but I pray I will see that some day.

CHAPTER 9

TRUE SALVATION AT LAST

Now that you've been warned about how the char-ismatic Antichrist will come to power, let's see what he does after the expiration of the three and one-half years of peace he will believe he has created.

After three and one-half years, there will be two beasts on the earth. The first one is political—the Antichrist—and the other will be religious—the false prophet. These two are men of Satan. By this time, I hope you've read the book of Daniel. God gave Daniel a vision of the latter days. Jesus gave his beloved disciple John an extended version of the same vision that God had given Daniel many years before. It was an amazing experience for me to see the correlation between the two books.

Recently, we have heard many politicians discussing the term, "New World Order." Daniel 7:23 and Revelation 13:7 tell us about this world government. According to the *Endtime* magazine, Mikhail Gorbachev made the term famous, and Pope

John Paul II referred to it repeatedly. It is interesting that this End Times one-world government was first introduced by a political leader and then continued to be used by a religious leader. At the United Nations World Summit held in September of 2005, 153 leaders converged for a huge surge forward into globalism. Many major developments toward a one-world government occurred at that summit.[4] According to Time magazine, Strobe Talbott said that "U.S. sovereignty will cease to exist in the 21st century and we will all answer to a single government authority."[5] How amazing a prediction is that? Eight years ago, this man essentially mentioned the plan that God left for us thousands of years before. Man only thinks he's smart! According to the Bible, the authority under which the United States and all other countries will eventually answer to is the man who one day establishes peace in Israel—the Antichrist.

In verse 3 of Revelation chapter 13, we read that the Antichrist will receive a fatal wound that will be healed: "The whole world was astonished and followed the beast." Verse 5 says: "(He) was given a mouth to utter proud words and blasphemies and to exercise authority for forty-two months. He opened his mouth to blaspheme God and to slander his name and his dwelling place and those who live in heaven. He was given power to make war against the saints and to conquer them. And he was given authority over every tribe, people, language, and nation. All inhabitants of the earth will worship the beast—all whose names are not written in the book of life belonging to the Lamb that was slain from the creation of the world. <u>He who has ear, let him hear</u>." Christians, are you listening?!

The Antichrist will bring peace to Israel, will be fatally wounded, and will recover. No one—except Christ—has ever been resurrected and ascended. Deceived people will believe that this man is the returning Christ—the Messiah. Jesus said in Matthew 24:4: "Watch out that no one deceives you. For many will come in my name claiming, 'I am the Christ' and will deceive many...Then you will be handed over to be persecuted and put to death, and you will be hated by all nations because of me. At that time, many will turn away from the faith....<u>And this gospel of the kingdom will be preached in the whole world as a testimony to all nations</u>, and then the end will come." Jesus continues in verse 23: "At that time, if anyone says to you, 'Look, here is the Christ!' do not believe it. For false Christs and false prophets will appear and perform great signs and miracles to deceive even the elect—if that were possible." Jesus told His disciples while He was on earth exactly what He later, in His resurrected body in heaven, would show John and ask John to write about in Revelation. Let's see some of those "signs and miracles" Jesus foretold.

Once the Antichrist has mankind firmly in his grasp, he will, according to Daniel 11:31, have "his armed forces rise up to desecrate the temple fortress and will abolish the sacrifice." Now, how can he do this if there is no temple? He can't; so we know that the temple must be rebuilt in Jerusalem. As I said before, Rabbi Chaim Richman, a member of the Israeli Sanhedrin, has stated that the third temple is ready for building. Once the sacrifice is abolished, Daniel tells us that the Antichrist "will set up the <u>abomination that causes desolation</u>. With flattery he will corrupt those who have violated the covenant, <u>but the people who know their God will firmly resist him</u>." (Also compare Daniel 8:23-25 with II Thessalonians 2:1-12 and Revelations 13). How do we know this is true? Turn to Matthew 24:15 where Jesus says: "So, when you see standing in the holy place <u>'the abomination that causes desolation', spoken of in Daniel</u>—let the reader understand ... there will be great distress unequaled from the beginning of the world until now." God will not allow a man of Satan to rule and reign from His temple. The final judgment of Satan begins at this point.

Revelation 13:11-18 tells us about a second man called the beast—the religious man of Satan. "He exercised all the authority of the first beast (the political Antichrist) ... and made the earth and its inhabitants worship the first beast, whose fatal wound had been healed." And (read this carefully, folks), "<u>he performed great and miraculous signs, even causing fire to come down from heaven to earth in full view of men.</u> Because of the signs ... he deceived the inhabitants of the earth. He ordered them to set up an image in honor of the beast ... he was given power to give breath to the image of the first beast (a clone?) so that it could speak and cause all who refused to worship the image to be killed." What about this did Jesus not predict while He was here on earth? Simply reread the previous two paragraphs. It is also important to note that a cloning takes place at this point. That could not have happened until recently when technology brought forth successful cloning. Did all of this happen in 70 A.D.? Was cloning available then? Wake up, churches! God's timing is perfect for His plans to be fulfilled. Are we close to this time of the end? What do you think?

The final verses of chapter 13 could also not have happened until recently: "He also forced everyone, small and great, rich and poor, free and slave, to receive a mark on his right hand or on his forehead so that no one could buy or sell—<u>creating a cashless society</u>—unless he had the mark, which is the number of the beast or the number of his name." At this point in God's plan, mankind must choose: Take the mark of Satan and eat or refuse the mark and perhaps be killed or starve to death but spend eternity with God. Notice that the mark is designated as only on the right hand or forehead—remember that. Before this time in history, how would such a mark be possible for the purchasing of goods? What has happened in the last few years to allow man to see the possibility of this? The answer: The development of computers and ID chips.

Articles from newspapers make the requirement of a mark easy to imagine. Implants of chips have been happening for a while now—all under the guise of good medicine, identity theft protection, and terrorist identification. In a newspaper article, columnist Rob Stein, wrote: "A microchip that can be implanted under the skin to give doctors instant access to a patient's records won government approval....Doctors would scan patients <u>like cans at a grocery store</u>."[6] Amazing, isn't it? I hope everyone sees that the vision our resurrected Lord gave to John regarding a "mark" as well as a cashless society is now humanly possible but became possible only recently. The article goes on to say: "It would obviously be possible to inject one of these into everyone."

In the post 9-11 world, we are already racing down the path toward total surveillance. Total surveillance is a necessary tool for the Antichrist to keep track of a world filled with people. Suddenly, cameras are appearing everywhere, aren't they? Just imagine, the Bible in the book of Revelation predicted total surveillance by a man called "Antichrist" thousands of years ago, but our denominational churches and their members, hanging on to tradition, heritage, and words of men—not God—may very well miss the deception of the Antichrist and might even, using human wisdom, accept the mark. How tragic ... and that is a tragedy that could be avoided if only man were to read the Bible in its entirety without denominational bias and with the Holy Spirit as the guide—something God clearly wants man to do.

Have you heard of RFID? These initials stand for Radio Frequency Identification tags. According to a newspaper article, RFID chips are "tiny silicon chips embedded in credit cards, passports and other everyday items (that) can transmit data about where you go, what you buy, and who you are. The devices include 'smart' car keys, no-swipe credit cards, prescription bottles, even shirts and shoes.... Critics say the tags and the signals they emit <u>are likely to be abused by people who would spy on your movements</u>."[7] Just who might spy on you? Might this be a perfect tool for a one-world government leader called the Antichrist to "see" you always and everywhere? Is God allowing man to create technology to defeat himself because man was disobedient to God? God promised, with a rainbow, that He would never again send a flood to destroy mankind, but He never said He wouldn't destroy mankind again. It appears to me that this time He is allowing mankind to destroy himself due to the lack of knowledge of biblical facts.

Detroit News staff writer Ed Garsten wrote: "There are now 40 million vehicles equipped with devices and sensors that record speed, direction, location and other data."[8] Do you have any doubt that the Antichrist can locate you anywhere on the earth if he comes to power soon?

According to *Perhaps Today*, the magazine of Jack Van Impe Ministries, Japan is, amazingly, considering the abolition of cash in its society.[9] Could the mark of the beast be far away? "*The Times Online* reports: 'Japan may start mulling the most radical monetary policy of all—the abolition of cash....'" How much more evidence do we need that the Bible, written thousands of years ago, is predicting the events in our world today? Will you be one who is so lacking in Bible knowledge that you will take "the mark" and, thus, belong to Satan for eternity? I pray not. How long has God given you to know better?

Let me now ask those denominational churches that teach that the events of Revelation took place in 70 A.D.: Is there any record of a man dying and being resurrected at that time, as the Bible says the Antichrist will do? Is there a record of anyone not being able to buy or sell unless he has a mark? Was a mark even possible for everyone at that time? Was cloning possible? Could man "see" everyone in the world in 70 A.D.? Satan has been an incredible deceiver of even our largest and most prominent churches, and church members have never questioned a thing they were taught—nor have their pastors or priests. People have simply believed the hierarchy of their churches and never read the Bible themselves to prove their churches right or wrong. Shame on us Christians!

The Antichrist is definitely coming. The computers and satellites that man built with pride will eventually become the telescope of the Antichrist. His Satanic eyes will be everywhere. He will deceive millions. Those who accept the mark will mock those who don't, but those who accept it have immediately purchased an eternal spot in Satan's kingdom, and many churches warned not one parishioner about this—not one! Revelation 14:9 says, "If anyone worships the beast and his image or receives his mark on the forehead or the hand, he, too, will drink of the wine of God's fury ... he will be tormented with burning sulfur in the presence of the holy angels and the Lamb. And the smoke of the torment rises forever and forever. There is no rest day or night for those who worship the beast or his image or for anyone who receives the mark of his name." Why will this happen? Because God gave mankind several thousand years to repent and believe and laid out His plan for the end of the world in the only book He ever wrote—the one which few have read. Remember God's words: "Men perish for lack of knowledge."

God will not allow the Antichrist to reign forever. God's timing is perfect. In Revelation 14:15, God says to his angel: "Take your sickle and reap because the time to reap has come, for the harvest of the earth is ripe. In Revelation chapters 15 and 16, God sends His final wrath upon the earth. He says in Revelation 16:15: "Behold I come like a thief! Blessed is he who stays awake....Then they gathered the kings together to the place that in Hebrew is called Armageddon" where God battles Satan and wins. Jesus and all of our loved ones—and even us if we die in Him or are raptured before this battle—will return to earth, to claim the victory, with all those who have died before this time and died believing in Jesus (See also Zechariah 14 and I Thessalonians 4:14). Evil is separated from good forever in this battle in Israel on what scholars believe are the plains of Megiddo.

Following the battle of Armageddon, Satan is bound for a thousand years (Revelation 20:2). John then says in verse 4, "I saw thrones on which were seated those who had been given authority to judge." Who are these judges? I Corinthians 6:3 says: "Do you know that the saints will judge the world? ... Do you not know that we will judge angels?" Those of us who are saved by the blood of Jesus will be the judges. Continuing in Revelation 20, we read: "And I saw the souls of those who had been beheaded because of their testimony for Jesus and because of the word of God. They had not worshiped the beast or his image and had not received the mark on their foreheads or their hands. They came to life and reigned with Christ a thousand years. (The rest of the dead did not come to life until the thousand years were ended). This is the first resurrection."

Revelation 20:7 says, "When the thousand years are over, Satan will be released from his prison and will go out to deceive the nations in the four corners of the earth ... to gather them for battle. In number they are like the sand on the seashore. They marched across the breadth of the earth and surrounded the camp of God's people, the city he loves. But fire came down from heaven and devoured them. And the devil, who deceived them, was thrown into the lake of burning sulfur, where the beast and the false prophet had been thrown. They will be tormented day and night for ever and ever." The ungodly trinity—Satan, the Antichrist and the false prophet—will spend eternity with those who, while on earth, chose Satan over God. What fools!

In chapter 20 of Revelation, the book of life is opened and the dead stand before the throne. "<u>They were judged according to what they had done</u> as recorded in the books. The sea gave up the dead and Hades gave up the dead.... Then death and Hades were thrown into the lake of fire. The lake of fire is the second death. If anyone's name was not found in the book of life, he was thrown into the lake of fire."

Revelation's final chapters, 21 and 22, are beautiful descriptions of the new heaven as well as a reminder that Jesus is coming soon. Revelation 22:20 says what we all should say, "Amen. Come, Lord Jesus."

Wow! At that point, I had, amazingly, come to the end of my year-long journey through the Bible. Thanks to the Holy Spirit, I really had read every word of every page of God's Word. I could hardly believe it! The year had gone by so quickly, and I was so grateful for the change that reading brought into my life—a change I could never have imagined when my journey began.

Today I continually ask the question, "Why me?" Why was I called out from among men and women in the Lutheran Church to read God's Word in its entirety? Who was praying for me? I know my sister and brother-in-law were. I know my paternal grandmother prayed for all of her grandchildren, but why was I the one who read the Bible and wrote this book? I can't answer those questions. I can, however, thank God over and over again. His call not only opened my eyes but opened the eyes of my husband. We could have received no greater gift than the gift of wisdom God gave us through the reading of His Word. That gift is available to you, too. All you have to do is pick up the Bible, dust it off, and read it from cover to cover remembering that there is nothing difficult in God's Word—nothing! One day, then, you, too, will join me in saying, "Why me, Lord? Why me?"

God does have a plan for the salvation of mankind whether it is the day we die, the day we're raptured, or the time we spend in the Tribulation. God will not allow man to live in a state of unrepented sin forever. As the world turns more and more away from God, those of us who love Him and believe that He sent His Son to die for us look forward to the eternity He has planned for us. In the meantime, our call is to witness and read His Word from cover to cover. He left His plan for man to know. Will you miss it because you didn't read? Does anyone now question why God in the Great Commission told us to "make disciples of all nations?"

CHAPTER 10

OUT OF THE DARKNESS,
INTO THE LIGHT!

When I finished reading Revelation, I knew I had to confront my pastor; and I also knew I had to share what I had learned with my congregation. My husband and I had attended this church for 17 years, and I felt a loyalty to the people. It was important to me that I share God's plan with them. In the end, though, I'm the one who became the learner. I learned far more about that church than I really wanted to know. We aren't always prepared for the plan God has for us, and there was absolutely no way I was the least bit ready for what He had in store for me.

Because our senior pastor was not available, I discussed my concerns and findings about Revelation with the assistant pastor. Having been a Lutheran for more than 40 years and, yet, realizing now that I had actually heard little of the Bible discussed in church, I felt I should find out why that was the case. I shared with the assistant pastor what I read in Revelation and asked why I had never heard any of this information before. He simply said he had something he wanted me to read and would get back with me. Shockingly, that "get back" came in the form of papers printed directly from the hierarchy of The Lutheran Church Missouri Synod. As before when I questioned Romans 11 and the senior pastor gave me paperwork from The Lutheran *Book of Concord*, I couldn't believe I was, once again, given a stack of papers from the Lutheran Church's position on Revelation with no willingness to sit down and simply go through the Bible with me. In Part III of this book, I finally will explain to you why both pastors handled my questions the way they did. Like me, I know you will be both shocked and amazed.

I got home that Sunday after my brief meeting with the pastor (who like the senior pastor before him never came back to me to see if I had any further questions) and began to read the information I had been given. First, I read that the Lutheran Church Missouri Synod believes that the Antichrist described in Revelation is actually the office of the Catholic papacy. I was stunned. That is biblically false, and now you know it's false, too. The Lutheran Church also believes that Jesus Himself is the New Temple rather than facing the reality that even today, the Jewish people have made priestly garments and edifices for the temple that will eventually be rebuilt in Jerusalem. The Lutheran Church condemns the fulfillment of the promises of Israel's restoration in 1948 or in the Jewish taking of Old Jerusalem in 1967.

The more I read, the angrier I became. This church—where I had been a member since birth and to which I had given my trust and my allegiance—did not rely on the Bible as it was written by God but the Bible as interpreted by the hierarchy of the Lutheran Church Missouri Synod. Like most Lutherans, my pastor believed it without question. I learned that this false approach to the Bible and, in particular, the Book of Revelation is well documented in a pamphlet entitled "The End Times—A Study on Eschatology and Millennialism". This is a report prepared by the Commission on Theology and Church Relations published by The Lutheran Church Missouri Synod. It is the doctrine to which all LCMS pastors must adhere. It's not about the Bible itself. It's about the Bible according to those who are or have been in charge of the church. How do you think Martin Luther would feel about this? Sounds like the very thing he stood against, doesn't it?

How is it that man could so wrongly interpret a Bible for hundreds of years that is so easy to read and understand? They have gotten away with it because of the manner in which churches train their seminarians and because they know the majority of Christians, including pastors, have never read and may never read the entire Bible. You and I can't question what we don't know. Let it be said that this is not simply a criticism of the Lutheran Church Missouri Synod, since basically all denominational churches are established on the interpretation of the Bible by men who claim to be learned and trained.

Have you checked your church lately? Has it been built on the "sand" of man's wisdom that Jesus biblically describes, or has it been built on the true Word of God with only the Holy Spirit as its guide? God will hold *each of us* responsible for knowing the Word. We won't be able to use as an excuse the fact that we simply believed that our pastor or priest read the Bible, knew it, and led us correctly. Each man is judged individually. Though the Bible says those who teach will be held to a higher standard, we can't use their unquestioning spirit as an excuse. We are to read our Bible and question our church. That is our responsibility. As President Ronald Reagan once said, "Trust but verify." Those of us attending denominational churches have simply trusted. We haven't even thought about verification, have we?

It became clear to me that any question I posed to my pastors would only be answered from church documents and not from the Bible. But I so badly wanted to remain Lutheran, so I had to ask just one more question of my senior pastor. I asked him about "the mark of the beast," which I have already explained fully in this book. Pastor told me that he would not believe anything about that mark unless I could find it in the Old Testament as well, because, according to him, everything in the New Testament—to be true—had to also appear in the Old Testament. I have often wondered if that is what the church really teaches or whether my pastor honestly believed I wouldn't find it in the Old Testament and that would end the discussion.

So, in prayer, I went searching. God alone led me to Exodus 13: 9, which says: "This observance will be for you like <u>a sign on your hand and a reminder on your forehead</u> that the law of the Lord is to be on your lips." Later in that same chapter, verse 16 says: "And it will be like a sign on your hand and a symbol on your forehead...." God had answered me. He had given me the words I needed. As you will recall, I told you previously that I believe that Pharaoh is the Antichrist of the Old Testament. The plagues of his time that rescued God's people are a foreshadowing of the Antichrist and the plagues that will, very soon, rescue God's people once again. After God led me to those passages in the Old Testament, I knew that both rescues involve "a sign on the hand and on your forehead."

I couldn't wait to see my senior pastor, not because I was right but because he told me he would absolutely believe me if I found a New Testament/Old Testament connection. So, I sincerely hoped that this would open the door to more conversations with him about the Bible. What I didn't expect is that as much as I personally like him, I would forever label him the "Doubting Thomas of 1989." I showed him the verses in Exodus. He looked at me and said, like Thomas did before Jesus, in His glorified body, openly displayed His nail scars, "I will not believe" —end of conversation. I was in shock. There was no doubt about it now. My pastor was clearly blinded by the indoctrination of his church and was biblically illiterate. By that time, I also knew he wasn't the only pastor in this category.

With my eyes suddenly wide open, I couldn't help lamenting for the young seminarians I had known so long ago as a student at Capital University and the congregations they have served. Over the years, I have either seen them or heard about them at Cap reunions. Actually, three of my roommates married seminarians from Capital. There is today no doubt in my mind that none of them—not one—had, as long as I had any contact with them, ever read the Bible from cover to cover. It is my prayer, though, that something has changed in their lives, and, at this point, perhaps they have read it. If not, they have spent a lifetime shepherding God's people with little knowledge of who God really is—and certainly very little biblical knowledge. They have been teaching what little Bible they know, and that teaching has come from the little they had been taught. Even that came from a denominational—not biblical—perspective. God must be very sad to think that even pastors haven't cared enough to completely read the one book He wrote. I will prove that in Part III.

The day my pastor said "I will not believe" forever ended my association with the Lutheran Church—or any denominational church, for that matter. Both of my pastors were stuck in and to doctrine created by men who have claimed authority over an earthly church, its seminaries, its publications, and its extended churches. The Bible would be taught as dictated by the Lutheran Church (and any other denominational church you can put in this sentence) and no other way. Not even the Word itself would be honored unless backed by the hierarchy of the church. I knew that I would never again be under the guidance of men rather than under the authority of God.

Unfortunately, my time at that church did not end with that meeting. First and foremost, I couldn't leave the Lutheran Church without my husband, and he stated emphatically that he wasn't leaving. Second, I felt I had an obligation to share my beliefs to the best of my ability with my 17-year church family. I just had to witness to them. Despite my best efforts, my husband got more and more frustrated with me, as did my fellow parishioners. All were die-hard Lutherans, as I had been. After three years of trying to make a difference for the Lord, I was sad and troubled. No one was going to listen to me—no one. Finally, in desperation, I prayed this prayer: "Lord, I can't do this any longer. If you want me to stay in this church, you will have to change my heart and give me peace. If you want me to leave, you will have to change the heart of my husband." Trying for three long years to witness on my own, I had finally left my frustrations with the Lord. Amazingly, and I do mean amazingly, that is when the change began—when I allowed God to "run the show" and not Gail. What happened next is God's very own miracle. I will never forget it. God was apparently waiting for me to need Him—to "let go and let God." He had taken me on an incredible journey through His Word. Now He was going to get the glory, as He should. He was going to do it all *His* way, and He let me watch His glory unfold.

Once a year, Lutherans celebrate Life Sunday. This is the time Lutheran pastors zero in on the horrors of abortion. As I said earlier, the year or so before, God had laid on my husband's heart the plight of the unborn. There was so much my husband wanted to do—and still does want to do—to turn this killing of babies around. He asked our senior pastor several times if he could inform our congregation about anti-abortion activities in and around the area so our church could get involved. There was never a positive response. At one point, our pastor said he couldn't talk too much about abortion in church because some people in our congregation had had abortions and such talk might bother them. My husband and I looked at each other in disbelief. Since when do one's activities determine a pastor's responsibilities to teach God's way to his congregation? Hurting someone's feelings now is better than making him or her ignorant for eternity, isn't it?

What I didn't know at that time, while I was struggling with my days in the Lutheran Church—in fact I only learned about it recently—is that God was not using just abortion to change my husband's heart, as I had long believed. He was also using a Christian radio station. My husband was working for General Motors at the time. His drive to and from work for 27 years, beginning in 1980, was approximately 35 minutes. During those drives, he began to listen to Detroit's very own Christian radio station WMUZ. The first host who caught my husband's attention was a man by the name of Al Kresta, a Catholic, who apparently had an amazing grasp of Scripture. But God chose Bob Dutko—who is still on the air today at WMUZ—to mightily grow my husband's faith in a way neither of us could have imagined. These men, along with Christian music hosted by WMUZ's Susan and the testimony and daily Bible verses offered by Robin Sullivan, added to my husband's knowledge and opened his eyes to the fact that churches other than—and perhaps more than—the Lutheran Church are biblically sound.

Between our pastor's stand on abortion—or lack thereof—and WMUZ radio, God was turning my husband's life more and more toward Him, and God didn't need me to interfere in the process. I only thought He did! How many times do we act on our own rather than "wait upon the Lord"? God tells us that those who "wait upon the Lord will rise up on eagle's wings." Not only were my husband and I rising up on eagle's wings, but we were also slowly soaring away from the Lutheran Church together. I just didn't know that.

In October of 1991, my husband asked our pastor to please make an announcement in church that an anti-abortion rally was being held in a nearby community. My husband was shocked, disappointed, and angry when our pastor said he wouldn't do it. Following that incident, my husband told me, and I was shocked, that we would be leaving that church. I was thrilled! It was clear to me, then, that when I took things out of my own hands and placed them in the Lord's Hands, God answered my prayer. I've never forgotten that. God doesn't need our guidance. He simply needs our obedience and our service.

Once I knew we were leaving the church, I wanted to leave the Lutheran Church altogether and attend a nondenominational church, but my husband told me he simply wasn't ready to leave the Lutheran Church. So, much to my dismay, we went in search of a new Lutheran Church home. This time I left that decision totally up to the Lord.

Visiting churches in search of a new church home was not something either my husband or I enjoyed. The question we often asked was, "Will we ever find a suitable place to worship?" That question was answered on a Sunday in April of 1992. Our daughter attended a Lutheran high school at the time and sang in the school choir. The choir visited and sang at area Lutheran Churches as a thank you for financial support given to the high school. This particular Sunday, my husband and youngest son had plans to attend a model railroad show. To accommodate everyone's schedule, my husband suggested he drive our daughter to church and attend the early service with our youngest son. I would bring our oldest son to the late service so I could drive our daughter home. We had no idea that day would change our lives forever.

The service itself was no different from any Lutheran service, but when the pastor preached the sermon, there wasn't a doubt in my mind that this man had read the Bible from cover to cover. I couldn't believe that the Lord had found a Lutheran pastor for us who was preaching a sermon from a book of the Bible that I had never heard preached before ... and he actually knew what he was talking about (how many of you would be able to discern that?). It was and is a moment frozen in time for me. I couldn't wait for my husband to get home that day and tell me his thoughts on the service. I knew that I had found my new church home—a place where God would be taught and honored by a man who had actually read the entire Bible. As soon as the door opened, I instantly knew by the smile on my husband's face that he felt exactly the same about the pastor. I was thrilled, and so was he. We had found our new church home!

Our last day at our old church was Confirmation Sunday in May of 1992. Confirmation in the Lutheran Church, as you may recall, is a time when, after training (that I now call indoctrination), one "confirms" his or her baptismal covenant of faith in Jesus Christ and *affirms the doctrine* of the Lutheran Church. It's a "now you're in" phenomenon—a "once saved, always saved" moment, as well as a "don't worry about your fig tree because you're in" moment. Our oldest son was being confirmed; and since he had gone through catechism, we felt he should go through the Confirmation service at our old church. By this time, however, I didn't believe in the ritual of Confirmation—and, in my opinion, a ritual it is.

The church sees it as someone's public confession of faith. The Bible does say that people must acknowledge their faith publicly, and I support that. The Lutheran Church, however, confirms young people just before they go to high school. There is no way that at that age kids are interested in anything beyond themselves. They are simply going through the motions of a church activity that their parents require of them. I was a very dedicated young girl to the Lord, but I can honestly say that I had little real understanding of what I was doing, even though the pastor who led me through catechism was excellent. I was simply too young and too much of a teen to think beyond the moment. Young teens shouldn't be required to speak publicly of their forever faith in Christ. That is an adult thing to do.

After our son's Confirmation, it was years before we returned to our old church for a visit. My husband and I were both happy in our new church home, and we loved and respected our new pastor. To this day, I tell that pastor—and others—that God used him to change my life in a way that forever sealed me to Christ. That pastor knew the Bible better than anyone I'd ever met, and he knew it down to the finest detail. He preached the Bible in a way that moved me every Sunday to search the Scriptures further. I told him one day that I could never understand how Abraham could take his son, Isaac, to be a living sacrifice—a burnt offering—for God. I knew I could never do that to one of my children. Not hesitating for a moment, pastor said it is because Abraham knew God well enough to know that Isaac would not be burned. I instantly knew pastor was right. My lifelong question had been so easily answered.

Another time, after my Baptist niece showed me that my version of the Bible was not accurate and I began to believe she could be right (many Baptist denominations insist that the only acceptable Bible is the King James Version), I asked pastor about that. He showed me immediately in the Bible where she was wrong. I marveled at pastor's biblical knowledge and still marvel at it today. My husband and I both thank God all the time that He moved us to be part of this pastor's church. (By the way, I would name our pastor, but he has asked to remain anonymous, fearing that he would himself receive glory rather than God).

My husband and I looked forward to going to church every Sunday. We loved the people at the church, too. We began to get to know one of the elders, and he eventually told us part of the story as to how pastor became the person he is now. This elder worked for General Motors, and he and some other members of the congregation began attending an interdenominational Bible study at work. As Lutherans, none of them had ever thought about reading the Bible from cover to cover but began to hear others in the group speak about what the latter called the "End Times." Soon the elder and the others began to read the Bible and saw for themselves what their fellow workers had seen. They came back to the Sunday Adult Bible classes at our church and shared their newly-found information. Pastor became very anxious about all the questions they asked every week and eventually asked the men not to come to Bible class anymore because they were disturbing the class. The men decided they would not leave the class, stating that they were members of the church and were allowed to attend any class they wanted to attend. They also told pastor that he should read the Bible for himself so he could answer their questions, and that is exactly what pastor did.

Like me, pastor was amazed at what was in the Bible that he never knew before. Later, he told me that the Lutheran seminary did not require him to read the entire Bible. I had never heard that before. I was shocked! How could that be? Surely he must be mistaken. How could someone become a pastor or priest in any church if he hadn't been required to read the Bible from cover to cover? I had a hard time believing that, but why would my pastor lie about something so important?

I began to think seriously about the seminarians I had known personally during my time at Capital University. It didn't take long before I knew that they could not possibly have read the Bible from cover to cover or they would have been excited about the new information they found, just as I had been. The fact that pastors and priests can graduate from seminary without having read the entire Bible began to sink deeply into my soul. That was when the very first hint took root that I might someday write a book and share that information with denominational Christians everywhere. Biblical illiteracy among pastors and priests was something I felt Christians needed to know, whether they believed me or not.

Once our pastor read and studied the entire Bible, he forgot how to be Lutheran. He saw exactly what I saw—that the Bible is full of truths never mentioned in the Lutheran Church. Like me, he wanted the people in his congregation to know the information from the Bible he now knew, and he hoped they would read the Bible for themselves and become enlightened. They were in the dark, though they didn't realize it, and pastor was fully aware that he was partially responsible for that. He had simply repeated the Lutheran doctrine that he had been taught—doctrine which, like most in denominational churches, has blindly been accepted without question.

Once pastor read the Bible, he began to preach it in its entirety rather than strictly adhering to doctrine. As he did that, people were uncomfortable. Pastor was preaching things they had never heard before. Instead of checking for themselves to see if what he said was or was not against the Bible, they simply hung on to Lutheranism and became angry with pastor. They nearly crucified him. It was a clear example of how biblical illiteracy leads to blind indoctrination. My husband and I witnessed what heritage and tradition can do to a wonderful man of God.

We remembered Jesus' return to his home synagogue in Nazareth. Instead of the people being open to listening, they rejected Him. Parishioners in our new church slowly began to take their concerns to the synodical office of the Lutheran Church. Those of us who had read the Bible were saddened that this congregation sought to remove a rare Bible-believing pastor via a synod that relied on doctrine more than on God's Word. Worst of all, I recognized that I, too, would have been one of them had I never read the entire Bible. Like the people of Jerusalem, I would have cried, "Crucify him" for daring to teach that which I couldn't defend. Little did the congregation realize that the only charge they had against this pastor was that he read the entire Bible and forgot how to be Lutheran, just as Jesus forgot to be Jewish.

Many wonderful things came out of a controversy that tore at the heart of an outstanding pastor and his family. That's what happens when God is in charge and directs one's life. First, and probably the best thing, is the fact that my husband recognized something was different about this pastor. While God had unblinded my doctrinal eyes through my reading of the Bible in its entirety, God had now unblinded my husband's eyes through what he saw a Bible-believing pastor going through. It was a wonderful unveiling. The other positive in the midst of sadness was the fact that a small group of us who supported the pastor became a church family in a way I hadn't experienced since my beloved days at Gethsemane Lutheran Church in the early 1950s. Our small but determined group loved and supported one another as well as the pastor and his family. We had meetings and prayed for God's wisdom and guidance, trusting God every step of the way. To this day, I count as special all those wonderful people whose lives touched mine in a remarkable way.

With the Lutheran congregation now divided between those who wanted a Lutheran pastor who taught only doctrine and not Scripture as it is written in its entirety and those who knew pastor was preaching the Word in its purity and were eager to learn from him, the handwriting was clearly on the wall. It was time for pastor to leave. What a painful time for him and his family. He had been raised Lutheran, attended Lutheran schools all his life, and attended a Lutheran seminary. With God's help, he had built successful Lutheran Churches. All he wanted to do now was teach the pure Word of God, apart from doctrine. No one would listen, however, and I knew just how he felt. Pastor knew, in his heart, that he should leave the church. He was no longer a young man, though. He was nearing retirement age. How could he start again? How could he meet his personal bills with little or no income? Those of us who believed in what he was doing continued to encourage him with our prayers and our tithes.

With courage that only the Holy Spirit can give, pastor made the gut-wrenching decision to finally leave the Lutheran Church and start a nondenominational church. Though he was eligible to retire, the Lutheran synodical leaders, to my shock, told pastor that he would not receive his pension unless he met the following criteria: He must not tell the congregation that he was leaving to start a new church. He could only say that he was retiring. Many of us felt that a church leadership with that much insecurity did not deserve such an honorable man. Looking back on it now, I honestly do not believe the church could have kept pastor from getting the pension he had earned; and I'm sure they knew that. Pastor, however, was taking a step of faith with no clue what was ahead of him, and that pension was important to him and his family. So, while he honored his word not to disclose the new church that was being formed, many of his supporters, including myself, simply called people and told them the truth. Many of those would later follow us to our new church.

Pastor officially retired from the Lutheran Church Missouri Synod one Sunday and two Sundays later, we were worshipping under his leadership in our new church home—the auditorium of a local junior high school. I still remember pastor sharing with us, after the fact, that he wondered if even a handful of people would be at that first service and felt he might have to supplement his income by washing cars to keep his family going. God knew better, though. When God directs our lives and we follow, He takes care of the rest.

To pastor's amazement—and ours—nearly 300 people attended that first service under the auspices and banner of a nondenominational church. We were all so thankful that such a God-fearing man who had faithfully served the Lutheran Church for so long and whose only fault was reading the Bible in its entirety received God's stamp of approval in regards to his future by the number of people who came to thank him and wish him well. Under pastor's leadership, this church continues to flourish.

One sad thing came in the form of a phone call from a relative, who was still very much a Lutheran. He let us know how unhappy he was that we left the Lutheran Church. We understood exactly where he was coming from. The attachment to a denominational church, as we look back on it today, is much like that of a cult, though the Lutheran Church is definitely not a cult. It is a stronghold of heritage and tradition going back generations, and that is true of all denominational churches. Family traditions and, in many cases, even family pride, have been for years wrapped around a denominational church.

Our relative was hurt. His words, however, closed the door for me forever on the Lutheran Church. He said he had done some checking into our pastor on the Internet, and the Lutheran Church Missouri Synod had declared that our pastor left the church to start a cult. I was so angry that I never checked that Web site. I knew that such an untruth would do me no good if I saw it. I also knew that if our relative was right about the content of the Web site, it was a sad commentary on the life of an incredible pastor who had done nothing more than read the entire Bible. That a church, if the story is true, could be so threatened by a pastor's leaving that it would willingly demean his character in such a horrific way would make me ashamed that I ever called myself Lutheran in the first place. I simply left that for God to handle; and when you consider how many members the Lutheran Church has recently lost, I believe God has handled it.

On Oct. 25, 2009, in a television sermon by Dr. D. James Kennedy taped before his death, he asked his congregation a question: "Are you a Protestant?" He continued: "Most people have no idea what the word 'Protestant' means or anything about the Reformation. They are simply born into the church they attend. They have no idea what the Gospel says and don't know if what is being preached is biblical or not." Dr. Kennedy's words couldn't be more profound. The so-called Christian world with its biblical illiteracy couldn't prove a pastor right or wrong if their very lives depended upon it. How about you? Do you know enough about the Bible to recognize the truth of what is being preached in your church every week? If not, when are you planning to get that Bible reading done?

It is important for me to again say that though I'm writing this book about Lutheranism, I have seen similar issues in other denominations. In Luther's day, people protected him from a certain death sentence when he nailed his 95 complaints against the Catholic Church to the door of the church in Wittenberg, Germany. The Catholic Church hierarchy was out to get Luther. Questioning a denomination or placing it in a disparaging light can elicit grave consequences. I saw that happen when Tim LaHaye and Jerry Jenkins wrote the *Left Behind* series. Their fictional, yet factual, portrayal of the Book of Revelation not only allowed 40 million people to better understand that book of the Bible, but it brought people to a saving faith as well. The denominational churches stepped forward quickly, however, to denounce the series. How sad—especially when the Revelation story was so well portrayed in these books and isn't even taught in the Lutheran Church.

Denominational blindness has thwarted God's plan for his church in a way that people who have never read the entire Bible can't begin to see. It isn't "God said it; I believe it; that settles it." It's "the church believes it; they teach it; I don't check into it but, by golly, if it was good enough for my parents and grandparents, it's good enough for me." But here's the question: Is it good enough for God, or does He expect more from us than resting on the beliefs of our family and our church?

My husband and I finally left the Lutheran Church for good and have never looked back or regretted our decision. My husband was even led to read the entire Bible himself. Isn't God amazing?! Together, we loved our new church and church family. We worshipped in the school for nearly three years until we could build a new church home. Those were three wonderful years. The "family" of believers grew not only in numbers but in Bible knowledge and genuine love and concern for one another.

Pastor's weekly sermons so riveted people that he was encouraged to bring them to be broadcast every Sunday on WMUZ radio. Pastor chose me to introduce that radio ministry, and he and I produced a radio show together on that Christian radio station for the next five years. Giving pastor a stage on which to share his incredible Bible knowledge was nothing short of a God-given privilege for me. One day, though, I believed the Lord was calling me to do something different for Him other than the radio broadcast. Thanks solely to God, pastor's life-changing radio ministry continues to be broadcast to this day, and people all over the metropolitan Detroit area are blessed with God's biblical message that weekly resonates through pastor, even motivating some who hear to worship God at pastor's church.

I will always be amazed by how many hours a day pastor studies the Bible—more hours per week than anyone I've ever known. He takes Old Testament stories, connects them to the New Testament, and then, to our daily lives. I doubt that I will ever meet another pastor like him. There just can't be two of him anywhere, though I sincerely hope there are. With God's guidance and direction, pastor was the influence that grew my faith and changed my life for Jesus in ways I could not possibly imagine. To this day, I tell pastor as often as I can how grateful I am that God placed him in my life, and my husband does the same. If, along life's journey, I never meet another pastor like him, I have met one whose Bible knowledge and insight will never be forgotten by me and many others. He is an amazing man of God to whom I will always be grateful. To God be the glory, pastor!

Our new church flourished. To date, there are two services on Sunday and a new building has been built to house Bible studies, fellowship gatherings, youth activities, and more. I couldn't be happier for such a wonderful man of God who stepped out in faith, not having a clue what was ahead, and made a difference in the lives of an incredibly large number of people. To think that I was privileged to know and appreciate him is one of God's greatest gifts in my life and that of my husband.

When pastor first told me he had never read the complete Bible in seminary, I questioned that. How could a seminary of any religion graduate a pastoral candidate without the assurance that he had not only read the entire Bible but that he had also studied it and was fluent in it? Would you ever go to a cardiologist who had studied only half of the circulatory system?

I had been raised to believe that pastors were better than the rest of us because they knew God's Word better, which only makes sense. Surely something was missing in what our pastor said. It would be important that I research it, and that research is the heart of Part III of this book. You won't believe what I learned about denominational seminaries and their churches in the United States. Prepare yourself for more of the Holy Spirit's eye-opening revelations and perhaps a God-blessed departure from the denominational church that has held you an arm's length away from Him for a lifetime.

Part III

"The truth shall set you free"

CHAPTER 1

DECEPTION IN THE DENOMINATIONAL CHURCH

It is my prayer that at this point, you have found things you never knew before within the Bible. If that's true, and I believe it is, you have to be asking yourself why you've been in the dark all this time. You have to be shocked that the Bible is not taught in its entirety in seminary. I certainly was. Reality is, though, that the responsibility for the problem rests first with you; second, with your church; third, with heritage and tradition that encouraged blind indoctrination; and fourth, with Satan—the greatest deceiver, according to the Bible.

Why am I laying the blame mainly on you? Because Jesus did not establish the churches as we know them today—man did. These churches have remained because you—and I—didn't read the Bible and haven't questioned whether they are totally biblical or not. We have placed our faith in churches established by men, not God. We don't question because we don't have the knowledge to do that, and we don't have that knowledge because we haven't read the Word. We have been deceived, and we allowed it to happen. I believe the following illustration might help you to see what you previously couldn't have imagined. See if you and your church are in this scenario.

Let's say that I have been hired by your local university to teach an in-depth analytical course on Ernest Hemingway's novel, *A Farewell to Arms.* My goal in this course is to make you a lifelong, committed fan of Mr. Hemingway, an avid reader of his novels, and an ambassador for his ideals and values. In the end, I hope you and I convince as many people as humanly possible that Hemingway is the greatest author of all times and that this book is the one everyone should read and build their lives on.

Now that I have you interested in taking my class, what are my qualifications to teach it? First, my parents, grandparents, and generations of family members before them loved Hemingway and spoke weekly about him, though none of them has ever read more than six chapters of any of his books. Their dedication to Hemingway led me to want to teach this class. Second, I attended the University of Michigan and earned a bachelor's degree with a minor in English. As a UM student, I was enrolled in a Hemingway class for two semesters. It was a survey class, and time didn't allow the professor to teach any Hemingway book in its entirety. We did read a few chapters of each book, and my professors admired Hemingway as much as my family did. The professors, in fact, admired him so much that they wrote several books about him and attended classes themselves on his writings.

In the class that I will teach, I plan to use the books written by these professors at least 60 percent of the time. If we are able to read portions of *A Farewell to Arms,* that will be fine; otherwise, we will rely on the expertise of the UM professors.

Though I have read only a few chapters of *A Farewell to Arms* myself—some of them many times over—I believe my family history and my college experience will make me the best professor you have ever had. I promise to place Hemingway's greatness in your heart forever so that you will want to be as much an ambassador for him as I am.

Now that you know all about my class and my qualifications, let me ask you this: How quickly are you running to your computers to sign up for my class? Hopefully, you aren't! In fact, I'd be concerned about you if you did. What's the problem? The truth is, you and I both know that I'm not the least bit qualified to teach the class. In reality, I'm only going to get you into my class if you share my love of Hemingway or if you believe that I'm an expert simply because I have the title "professor" before my name—a title you feel you have no reason to question mainly because you know so little about Hemingway yourself that anything you hear will be a learning experience for you.

Believe it or not, the above scenario illustrates exactly what has happened in the life of your church and your role there. Though you wouldn't consider attending my Hemingway class—and good for you— you and millions like you, each and every week, attend a denominational church under exactly the same set of circumstances, and no one thinks a thing about it. How do the Hemingway class and the church you attend compare? First, you are undoubtedly attending the church because it is familiar to you. Your parents, grandparents and extended family all attend either the same church or the same denominational church that you attend. In some cases, you may even experience a mini family reunion every Sunday, and that helps your family feel warm and cozy there. You may have been baptized, confirmed, and even married there. Your parents and grandparents may have been buried from that church. Also, you can go to any church of that denomination in any city around the world and feel comfortable because churches of the same denomination basically do things the same way. For many of you, the real reason you are attending your church is that it fits into your "comfort zone." The first question I would ask you, though, about this "comfort zone" is: Does Jesus want you to feel comfortable in your church, or does He want you to grow in your faith and in biblical knowledge so that you can be His witness wherever you go?

Second, like my scenario showed, it's very likely that your parents, grandparents, extended family, and even you have never read more than a few books or chapters of the Bible, though you may have read those few books or chapters numerous times during your church-attending years. That's because denominational churches tend to teach from the same books of the Bible year after year after year. Some books of the Bible are never or rarely taught in your church. I would venture to say that many of your family members who have died never read the Bible from cover to cover. You may be arguing with me at this point, but you need to open your Bible and count the chapters you have read. In reality, you can't adequately discuss what you haven't read, can you? If you do get into a biblical discussion, which I know is rare, you speak only in the words of your denomination without regard to whether they are right or wrong because you've never thought they *weren't* right. You probably use the excuse that you don't discuss religion or politics, but that is Satan's greatest lie in your life and in the lives of millions of other Christians. Satan has stopped—dead in its tracks—the Great Commission Jesus left us: To "go into all the world making disciples of all nations." We have hidden behind the words "I don't discuss religion" and, thus, have disobeyed God and have limited His plan for the salvation of mankind. Satan is loving it, and He has won, too!

The real reasons I believe you don't witness are: 1) You're afraid of what others will think of you, 2) you lack Bible knowledge, or 3) as a result of blind indoctrination, the people you know have been baptized and, thus, you believe they're saved. Neither "scared" nor "a lack of Bible knowledge" nor "blind indoctrination" is a viable excuse in the eyes of God for not witnessing. Paul told us that we "can do all things through Christ who strengthens us," and that strength comes from putting on "the full armor of God," which is the Word.

At this point, I hope you're questioning your long-held loyalty to a church rather than to the Word, as well as your lack of witnessing. Yes, the sins of not reading the entire Bible and ill-placed loyalty to a manmade church belong first to you, as they did to me. It wasn't until the Holy Spirit revealed that sin to me that He also opened my eyes. I often wonder if He ever would have revealed the truth to me had I not chosen to read the only book ever left for me to read. II Cor. 3:16-18 says: "<u>When one turns to the Lord, the veil is removed</u>. Now the Lord is the Spirit; and where the Spirit is, there is freedom. And all of us, with unveiled faces, seeing the glory of the Lord as though reflected in a mirror, are being transformed into the same image from one degree of glory to another; for this comes from the Lord, the Spirit." James 4:8 says: "Draw close to God and God will draw close to you."

The truth is, I read the Word and then met the Lord—personally—for the very first time. I knew very little about Him before then. I only thought I knew Him. I found the sin of my denominational church in the Word, and then the Holy Spirit laid the blame squarely on me for allowing my church to guide me rather than the words of my God. It is a sin that required my deepest repentance and led to the writing of this book.

Now that you are beginning to see your wrong (at least I hope you are), the blame doesn't rest *entirely* with you. The leaders of your church are also responsible for your biblical illiteracy. They, too, have held onto the indoctrinated idea that they have all the answers and that their church is right. Yet, most of them haven't read the Bible from cover to cover—neither the church hierarchy nor the pastors or priests—but vehemently support church doctrine out of heritage, tradition, and the little Bible knowledge they have. Again, are you as shocked as I was to learn that my pastor, the leaders of the Lutheran Church, and those in seminaries— students as well as professors—have, for the most part, never read the entire Bible?

If you read magazines and books printed by your denomination, you'll be reminded often how wonderful your church is. Regrettably, you'll hear biblically only what that church wants you to hear. There will be great rebuke of those who stray from what the church teaches. Remember what the synod put my pastor through when he read the Bible in its entirety and questioned the doctrine of the Lutheran Church? Believe me, this book will garner a heap of criticism from denominational leaders. Why? Ignorance, fear, heritage, and tradition make men and women loyal to that which they should abandon, and the fear of that abandonment makes the church uncomfortable, defensive, and attacking.

So, what is the church's responsibility in all of this? Think about the following: One of the reasons you would not attend my class on Hemingway is because I told you I had only read a few chapters of the book that was the subject of the class. I also told you that I had read those chapters numerous times, however. You are intelligent enough to realize that no one can teach a book that they haven't read and studied in its entirety. Yet, that is how pastors and priests have been and are being taught at denominational seminaries. If you attend a denominational church this Sunday, chances are your pastor or priest has not read the entire Bible. Why? They weren't required to do so in semi-nary or anywhere else. How, then, can they teach it to you? They do that using their incomplete knowledge of the Bible as well as using publications from their denomination—and they've never questioned a thing. This is, of course, not true of every pastor or priest—just most of them.

The important issue to denominational churches is that the pastors or priests indoctrinate their congregants into *that* religion. Churches make sure doctrine is the trump card that is taught to the people. Such teaching has kept people in churches for centuries—churches that don't teach the entire Bible—and they have succeeded, at least until recently. Have you noticed the incredible growth of nondenominational churches in America? Have you wondered why? Many Christians—thank you, Jesus—have come to know the truth that I now know and have left the churches of their "comfort zones" behind. Once I knew the truth about what is really taught—and, more importantly, not taught—in denominational seminaries, my life was turned around. It is my prayer that "truth" does the same for you. I pray "the truth will set you free."

Let me begin to prove to you that denominational seminaries don't teach or require reading of the entire Bible. On June 15, 2008, I interviewed a pastoral candidate who was then attending Concordia Lutheran Seminary. What a fine young man—so innocent and so dedicated. He will be a wonderful asset to the Lutheran Church Missouri Synod, but will he, as a denominationally indoctrinated pastor, be an asset to the Lord? In some ways, yes, and in some ways, no. He was the perfect person to interview—open, honest, friendly, knowledgeable, and excited about his future in the church. He knew I was writing a book but was still candid with me. (I will not reveal the identity of this young seminarian because of the repercussions he would undoubtedly experience if his name were revealed.)

This young man first explained to me that the seminary adopted a new curriculum in 2006. Candidates are taught that they are "rightly called," meaning that God uses the *church* to call a candidate. Churches, the candidates are told, are the instrument by which God finds the pastor to serve the people. Isn't it funny that Jesus literally ran away from the established church at the time—the Jewish synagogue—and openly criticized it, while finding the "pastoral candidates" He was looking for? He actually dared to "buck" the system at that time. Jesus didn't choose the rabbis or their protégés to spread God's message of salvation. He chose fishermen. Jesus did that because those "pastoral candidates" learning under the Jewish rabbis were not hearing the truth but were, instead, being indoctrinated into the Jewish faith. Why then would God today suddenly use churches divided by denominational barriers of indoctrination and biblical illiteracy to select pastoral candidates? That doesn't make an ounce of sense to me nor should it to you. The Bible says God calls people to His service—any service in His name—because He alone has distributed the gifts and talents to them for His purposes, and He knows exactly how He wants each person to use them. I believe some of His greatest workers have not necessarily been members of a denominational church or synodically trained.

Do you remember David of the Bible—the shepherd boy? Incredibly, of all the able-bodied available men whom God could have selected to kill the giant Goliath, He chose, instead, David, the shepherd boy; and David had only a sling shot with which to do the job. Mission accomplished! In that story, God knew that the real giant was David. He knew that because He created David with the gifts and talents needed to accomplish His purposes. Interestingly, when others saw a shepherd boy, God saw a king. That is still true today. Often, nondenominational pastors are criticized by denominational clergy and laity: How dare they pastor without seminary training! Isn't that what the people of Nazareth thought of Jesus when He spoke in their local synagogue? What was Jesus' response? He spoke of their lack of faith. Isn't God capable of creating, molding, and teaching His pastoral candidate through the one Book He wrote rather than through any seminary built by man? Besides, from my research, it seems seminaries have a lot to learn about teaching the Bible versus the doctrine of man.

After you read the rest of my interview below of the young Lutheran seminarian, I hope you'll see that the nondenominational pastor trained only by the Holy Spirit through the Bible just might be better qualified to pastor than anyone who attended a denominational seminary. Think about this: Is God the best teacher of his future pastors or are seminary professors—sinful men—the best teachers? God sees in a man what others do not see. Perhaps when any of us criticize a pastor because he didn't go to seminary, we need to ask ourselves: While others see an ordinary non-seminary trained pastor in the pulpit, what does God see?

The pastoral candidate continued the interview by saying the curriculum at Concordia is divided into two parts, "practical" and "exegetical." Practical includes caring, preaching, counseling, missions and evangelism. Exegetical is the teaching portion of the seminary. He said they learn Greek and Hebrew as well as a great emphasis on the Gospels—Matthew, Mark/Luke (taught together) and John. They use the Greek text all week in class, and <u>60 percent of their textbooks are written by professors</u>. What?! Stop and ponder that for a moment. Go back to the Hemingway scenario and see what you think about this. Compare the pastoral candidate's study time of the Bible with his study of textbooks written by professors. More than half of the time in seminary is consumed with textbooks written by sinful men—people like you and me who simply have been published. Why not read those books on one's own time but study the Bible alone in seminary? Where would God put the emphasis?

What church worth its weight in gold would place more emphasis on writings by seminary professors than the one and only book written by a perfect God? What could be more proof of manmade doctrine over the Bible in a church than that? Believe me, no book is used in any seminary that isn't first approved by the publishing company of that denomination. It must meet strict standards of adherence to the beliefs of the denomination. Instead of the Bible, pastoral candidates concentrate on the opinions of sinful, indoctrinated men. Something is very wrong with that scenario.

What an opportunity for Satan to work and stop Jesus' Great Commission dead in its tracks! It is doctrine that prevents Christians from working together for Godly causes. Yet, just how much of that doctrine in any church—not just the Lutheran Church—is truly biblical? When was the last time anyone checked that doctrine against the Bible?

The Lutheran pastoral candidate went on to say that by the time he is ordained, he will also have been taught the first five books of the Bible—known as the Torah—the major and minor prophets (though not in depth), Psalms, and the Epistles of the New Testament. There are 66 books in the Bible. Are you getting the picture here? How many biblical books are never—or only briefly—read by a pastoral candidate the entire time he is at Concordia Seminary? Why isn't this young man concerned about that? The answer is: He's indoctrinated! And, guess what? The Lutheran Church is not alone in this biblical neglect. I'll prove that to you later in this book.

According to the candidate, another important book taught in the seminary is the *Book of Concord.* Do you remember from previous chapters how often that book was used to answer the biblical questions I raised in my own Lutheran Church? Every time I asked one of my pastors a question, he got the answer from the *Book of* Concord. Do you understand why I was so shocked back then? That book is the Lutheran Church's interpretation of the Bible. Instead of learning the truth *from* the Word, pastors believe the truths *of* the Word are in the *Book of Concord*—a book written by man. Isn't there a commandment that says: "Thou shalt have no other gods before me?"

After my years of experience with the church, I have come to believe that the *Book of Concord* is a god of the Lutheran Church Missouri Synod. It's only logical that if pastoral candidates don't study and understand the whole Bible, how can they possibly know God's truths, let alone teach it to their congregants? And why are they accepting the Bible according to the *Book of Concord?* The answer once again is blind indoctrination. I know; I was there. Lutheran seminaries aren't creating followers of Jesus or witnesses for Him. They are creating followers of Luther and a doctrine called "Lutheran."

I specifically asked this young man if the Book of Revelation is read. "No," he said, "it is not read. If you want to know about it, you can come back to the campus to take classes following graduation." Folks, how often do you think that happens? Once ordained, pastors become very busy people—balancing the many needs of their church with their own, often growing, families. They earn little money and probably have a mountain of debt from four years at a private school and four more years in the seminary. When do you think they'll go back to the college campus to study Revelation? Do you honestly think God wants any seminary to leave out of its curriculum even one word He wrote, let alone entire books?

Remember Revelation 1:3 says, "Blessed is the one who reads the words of this prophecy, and blessed are those who hear it and take to heart what is written, because the time is near." God absolutely told all of us to read Revelation, and those who read it will be blessed. Then, He asked us to place in our hearts what is written. Knowing this, why would any seminary disobey God by not teaching Revelation and not requiring its seminarians to read, study, and know that book and all the other books in the Bible, for that matter? More importantly, why would mature pastors not read it? Are you still sure you want to remain in your doctrinal church that doesn't teach the whole Bible?

Is there any lack of understanding now among you as to why Revelation was not taught—and only rarely mentioned—in any Lutheran Churches I've attended? People don't teach what they don't know, do they? That's why you chose not to enroll in my Hemingway class. Even if a pastor came back to campus to take a class on Revelation, would it be taught doctrinally, or would it be taught through the words of the Holy Spirit? If the former is your answer, you are beginning to understand the truth.

The candidate said that he and the others receive what is called the *Pastoral Care Companion* book, and it goes everywhere with them. It contains services, prayers, etc. He also said the candidates go on Field Education for six quarters—something like student teaching. They must know Greek before entering the seminary and Hebrew before being allowed to go on vicarage—a year spent in a congregation under the watchful eye of a supervising pastor. He stated the importance of the Augsburg Confession of 1580 and noted that *Luther's Large Catechism* is mostly for pastors. How important do you think either the Augsburg Confession or *Luther's Large Catechism* is to God since they were written by men—particularly if the Bible hasn't been read or studied in its entirety? Who's receiving the glory here?

To my surprise, the candidate told me—first time I ever heard this—that Lutherans believe children even in the womb have faith. Apparently that is why their parents and Godparents can speak for them at infant baptism. Where is the womb faith of a child—or, for that matter, even infant baptism—found in the Bible? I haven't found either of them anywhere in Scripture. It does say that God knew us before He created us in the womb, but it does not say that He gave us faith in the womb. And never forget—God baptized Jesus as an adult and dedicated Him as a baby. What example do you think He wants us to follow—the one He designed or the one the church designed?

What you've just read is a summary of more than three hours of an interview with the Lutheran pastoral candidate. Since I had already read the entire Bible several times and I knew he had not, it was difficult for me not to say, "You're a wonderful young man who genuinely wants to serve the Lord, but you have no idea what you're doing because you don't know the Bible. You are simply a walking robot for a denomination, and the only thing you'll teach your congregants is what you yourself learned—blind indoctrination."

The young man told me that pastoral candidates must take a vow to teach only pure doctrine of the Lutheran Church Missouri Synod. Are you now at all surprised by that? I certainly wasn't. After all, what better way to keep a pastor away from anything that might make him question the church? Now you know why turning the life of a Lutheran pastor away from doctrine and toward the Bible would be a miracle. You can also imagine why I have such great and continual respect and admiration for that one special Lutheran pastor in my life who experienced just such a miracle, walking away from 25 years as a Lutheran pastor. He was led by God to change my life, my husband's life, and the lives of many, many others. He was one courageous, God-led man. He walked away from manmade vows and followed the Holy Spirit. How I wish there were more denominational pastors like him, and there would be if more read and studied the entire Bible with the Holy Spirit and without indoctrination by a denomination. As soon as our pastor did that, he left denominational indoctrination behind. My prayer is that at least some denominational pastors will read this book, then read the entire Bible, and, finally, will boldly question their church's hierarchy. What a difference that would make. Maybe there would even be a second Reformation!

If I were a pastoral candidate and was not required to read the entire Bible in seminary, I would ask why, wouldn't you? Why haven't these candidates asked? It's incredible to me. At the same time, I have to remember that as a devoted Lutheran, I never—until I read the Bible—questioned anything either. I didn't question because I didn't know enough to do so, and I had no idea pastors and priests weren't required to read the entire Bible. I simply assumed they had all read it. I'll bet you assumed that, too. In fact, I'll bet you *believed* they read the entire Bible, as I did. How do you feel now that you know the truth?

One day my husband asked our wonderful, God-led ex-Lutheran pastor why he left the Lutheran Church. Pastor gave these reasons: 1) Doctrinal differences. He said he began listening to good teachers like John MacArthur, Vernon McGee and Charles Stanley. Their faith, though not Lutheran, led pastor to a hunger for God's Word. He learned to take the Bible literally and realized more and more that there was no record of infant baptism in Scripture. He also began to see the emphasis on Jesus' "real presence" in the bread and wine of communion as just a carry over from the Catholic Church. It became clear to him that he had to teach what Scripture says. "It boiled down to this—when God reveals His truth, you can't ignore it. You can't pretend you don't know it and go on with life. That would have been intellectually dishonest and not in keeping with God's will." 2) The people who came to his Lutheran Church and didn't believe the Catholicisms that had come into the church were treated like second-class citizens. Nevertheless, they were and are wonderful, God-fearing people who were accomplishing great things for the Lord. 3) God began moving him several years earlier when he began to rethink some aspects of Lutheran doctrine.

God blessed our pastor greatly as time went along. As a member of this man's congregation, it will forever be amazing to me that he was moved to leave the church of his heritage, his comfort zone and his calling. The truth for the rest of us is that once you read and study the entire Bible without doctrinal hindrances but with the Holy Spirit's enlightening, you can't possibly remain Lutheran ... or probably any other denominational religion either.

Lutherans' reading of the Bible is clouded by doctrine since they learn doctrine first. Pastors know Lutheran doctrine better than they know the Bible. For generations, people have become addicted to Lutheranism, and that is true of all denominations. Families are addicted to Catholicism, to Methodism, to Presbyterianism, to Baptistism, etc. It is religion first, Bible second. A denominational Christian who disputes this is, I believe, simply in denial.

While working recently for a newspaper as a typesetter/proofreader, an article was placed in the paper that said the following: "The Lutheran Heritage Foundation, an international mission organization, is celebrating its 15th anniversary. LHF was founded with a mission to translate, publish, distribute, and intro-duce <u>Lutheran materials around the world</u>. To date, the organization has translated and published *Luther's Small Catechism* and *The Book of Concord* into more than 50 languages."[10]

Let's stop and give thought to what we have just read. It was Jesus who told us to "go into all the world and make disciples of all nations." Nowhere did He say, "Make everyone Lutheran, Catholic, Baptist, etc." In fact, it is biblically clear that He was not interested in such a thing. LHF, though, seems to want to make everyone Lutheran, and that's a major reason why Jesus' Great Commission has not been fulfilled by most churches. Man has narrowed the choices. With Jesus, there's only one choice, and it has nothing whatsoever to do with denominational religion. Besides, I say once again, why is it necessary to translate Luther's Small Catechism and The Book of Concord? Isn't the Bible all one needs? Show me in the Bible where God wanted us divided into denominations. Show me where God wanted us to be Lutheran, Catholic, Baptist, Episcopal, Presbyterian, etc. God wanted us to simply be biblically trained not denominationally indoctrinated.

In his book *Fearless,* Max Lucado speaks of his denominational interpretation of Christ and the new Christ he discovered as he grew in faith. He says, "I once reduced Christ down to a handful of doctrines. He was a recipe and I had the ingredients...<u>arrogant certainty becomes meek curiosity</u>. Define Jesus with a doctrine or confine Him to an opinion? By no means."[11] Like Mr. Lucado, I finally discovered the freedom to know the real Jesus after I read the Bible. No denomination would ever again prevent me from following the Jesus I had never known before—the one no longer placed in a box by those who have never read the entire Bible themselves but have hung onto truths they robotically followed without research of their own. Be honest with yourself now. Is that what you, too, have done?

It is important to see what can happen when a denominational church fails to teach the entire Bible. In 2006, my husband and I received a copy of *The Lutheran Witness*—a magazine published by Concordia Publishing House in St. Louis, MO. A statement on the back cover of the magazine says that it is the "official periodical of The Lutheran Church—Missouri Synod." Two articles in that magazine immediately caught my eye. The first was called "Whose Land Is It?" by a professor, who was, at the time (and may still be) an associate professor of exegetical theology at Concordia Seminary in St. Louis. The other was entitled "We Are Needed—Are Lutherans afraid to take on the world?" and was written by the director of the Concordia Seminary Institute on Lay Vocation in St. Louis and the Concordia Center for Faith and Journalism in Bronxville, NY.

The basic purpose of the first article is to dispute Israel's claim to ownership of its land and also to dispute the nondenominational view of Revelation and those biblical books which expound upon things like the rapture, the 1,000-year reign of Christ, etc. While the professor's words are undoubtedly doctrinally correct, they are not biblically correct. Throughout Scripture, it's clear that God gave the land to which He sent Abram to the Israelites. In fact, God tells mankind throughout the Bible that Israel is to be supported and also states that countries that do not support Israel will be punished. Jeremiah 30:16-23 says: "In that coming day, all who destroy you (Israel) will be destroyed... when I bring you home again from your captivity and restore your fortunes, Jerusalem will be rebuilt on her ruins...I will multiply my people and make of them a great and honored nation. Their children will prosper as they did long ago. I will establish them as a nation before me and I will punish anyone who hurts them." "And the Lord will send a plague on all nations that fought against Jerusalem" (Zechariah 14:12). This rhetoric from the Lord in regards to His restoration of Israel and His punishment of those who hurt that nation is prevalent throughout Scripture, but those who are doctrinal rather than biblical will undoubtedly miss them. It looks like the professor may be one of them.

He writes in his article that "when Jesus speaks about the land (of Israel) in Luke 19:41-44, He makes no reference to it ever being restored to the Jews."[12] As seen in the previous paragraph, that is completely untrue. If Jesus is God, as the Bible teaches, and if He was present at creation, as the Bible teaches, and if every word of the Bible is God-breathed, as the Bible teaches, then Jesus knew the words of Ezekiel 37, verses 12-14: "This is what the Sovereign Lord says, 'O my people, I am going to open up your graves and bring you up from them; <u>I will bring you back to the land of Israel</u>....I will put my Spirit in you and you will live, <u>and I will settle you in your own land</u>." Ezekiel was speaking directly to the Jewish people here. Then, there is Amos 9:14-15: "I will bring back my exiled people Israel; they will build the ruined cities and live in them.... <u>I will plant Israel in their own land never again to be uprooted from the land I have given them</u>."

Why is this professor disputing these—and other—direct teachings in the Bible? There are, I believe, two reasons. First, the Lutheran Church teaches that any time the word "Israel" appears in the Bible, people are to replace it with the word "church." But, "Where does it say that in the Bible?" This entire concept is a distortion from the truth in Scripture. Second, it is doubtful that this professor has ever read and studied the entire Bible without a denominational bias, if he has ever read and studied the entire Bible at all! His attendance and professorship at a Lutheran seminary is all the support we now need for that statement.

The truth is that Israel became a sovereign nation again on May 14, 1948. Jesus knew that would happen, but He expected us to read and study the entire Bible and not portions of it so we would know it, too. If pastors, professors, priests, and even you and I have never been required to read and study the entire Bible, all of us will believe anything our church teaches in regards to what the Bible says and doesn't say. There is no doubt that devoted Lutherans definitely believe the words of this professor without question. His words represent biblical illiteracy, however, and this deception by the church has been going on for generations, not because churches want to deceive but because they have believed the message passed down from generation to generation that their church, and only their church, has all the answers.

In the September 2009 "Levitt Letter," an article by Zola Levitt supports the biblical illiteracy of denominations. He writes: "A Methodist (or any denominational church) may deeply believe in our Lord, may study Scripture, may in every way conform to the biblical image of a Christian, but his denomination, in supporting the Palestinian side on the Israel question, is simply dead wrong. One could not have even a passing acquaintance with Scripture and hold so unbiblical a position toward the Promised Land and the Chosen People.... Some churches simply do not teach Scripture. Their members are in the dark about such crucial topics as Israel and prophecy."[13] There is nothing I could personally add to this. Zola Levitt has said it all. A professor's dedication to Lutheranism has kept him blind to the truth of Scripture, and he isn't alone in that blindness. As long as denominationalists hold onto their church rather than the biblical words of their God, I believe God will allow them to live in blindness.

No church or no person has all the answers; but, you and I, as well as seminarians, have been, and many still are, victims of a great deception. This is caused by those who have refused to question the teachings of their church against the Bible because they themselves are biblically illiterate. Hasn't Satan been doing an awesome job?

In his article, the professor also discusses the land of Palestine, but his timeline fails to add the most important detail. The Roman emperor Hadrian in 135 A.D. renamed Israel "Palestine," scattered the Jews as slaves throughout the Roman Empire, and, thus, took the God-given land of Israel away from the Israelites. Palestinians then falsely inherited the land—an extremely important fact that the professor either doesn't know or simply left out of his discussion. Clearly, though, what man took away from God's chosen people, God will one day restore. The transfer of that land is a historical fact, but the restoration of that land is a biblical fact.

Many Americans don't realize just how close Adolph Hitler came to winning World War II. Had he succeeded and occupied Western Europe, Great Britain, and the United States, as he planned, do any of us really believe that our parents or grandparents would simply have said, "Well, Hitler won that war fair and square. We're now Nazi Germany instead of the United States?" That would never have happened. Our families would have fought and would have taught us to fight to reclaim our land. The Jews have been taught exactly the same thing—and more power to them. They fought even through their own extermination to return to the land God gave them—the land the Bible asserts is rightfully theirs.

God's land did not belong to the Roman Empire and was not theirs to give away. It definitely does not belong to the Palestinians. The professor is biblically off base on this one. He should, as a Christian, be totally unrelenting in his support of Israel's right to exist. God said He'd punish the nations that don't support that right. Why would this professor teach and write something that is so antithetical to the Bible? Because he is blindly indoctrinated, of course!

The second article is just about as Lutheran as anyone can get. It purports that Lutherans should run for political office. I couldn't agree more, but it isn't Lutherans who should do that alone. All Christians should run for public office, or, logically, our government will be atheistic, agnostic, or simply lukewarm. Have you, as Christians, seen any evidence of that lately?

The article asks the question: "Where is (Martin) Luther?"[14] What the world really needs is not the Luther of the 1500s but a 2010 Luther or, better yet, many Luthers—people who have studied the Bible in its entirety without a doctrinal bias and who can bring Spirit-filled knowledge to the church and the nation. The eyes of Martin Luther were opened *because he studied the Bible*, and that reading dispelled the doctrine he had been taught. There is no other reason.

Once he realized that, he acted. Though everyone had the same Bible, it was Luther's reading of it that changed the course of history. However wonderful that was, nearly 500 years have passed. What Lutheran has gone beyond Luther's 1500s knowledge? Lutherans need to read the entire Bible, and they also need a 2010 Luther.

Baptism and Confirmation are just the beginning of one's walk with Jesus, and not the finality of it. There has to be growth. I remember what my Lutheran pastor said the day I was confirmed: "<u>Grow</u> in grace and in the <u>knowledge</u> of your Lord and Savior Jesus Christ." Just how do we do that? Do we only go to church on Sunday to achieve that? Do we attend all the social events in the church to achieve that? Do we serve the church in every capacity to achieve that? Or do we study the Bible in its entirety and, loaded with knowledge and a newly-found personal relationship with Jesus Christ, fulfill—or at least attempt to fulfill—the Great Commission? Lutheran indoctrination is not biblical indoctrination—not even close!

The article says that "Lutherans have it all—the right doctrine, even the right institutions."[15] I greatly appreciate this cheerleading; and if one has read and studied the *whole* Bible without doctrinal bias, one might be able to make such a claim. If not, and I suspect the author has not, what is it about heritage and tradition that makes *any* religion "right"? How would he begin to know that his church has "the right doctrine"? What has he compared it to? Why does man need "doctrine" at all? Why don't we just use the Bible as our guide? If the Lutheran Church is so "right," why is it losing members? Might its lack of witnessing have anything to do with that? For that matter, why are all denominational churches losing members in droves to nondenominational churches? Maybe the Bible itself has become more popular than the doctrine developed by man. Wouldn't that be wonderful?!

Deception goes on in denominational churches today, just as it has for generations, and no one questions it. When was the last time you questioned something in a periodical you received from your church? How many Lutherans do you think questioned the articles by either professor? I don't know about others, but my letters to them went unanswered.

Before man holds onto doctrine in the Lutheran Church or any other denominational church, he should consider the words of Jesus just before He ascended into heaven: "When He, the Spirit of truth (the Holy Spirit), comes, He will guide you into all truth. He will not speak on His own; He will speak only what He hears, and He will tell you what is yet to come. He will bring glory to Me by taking from what is Mine and making it known to you" (John 16:12-14). All seminaries should teach the Bible and only the Bible. Jesus told us in John that we will receive from the Holy Spirit—not from the church—what He knows so that we, too, will know. The very idea that 60 percent of the curricula of Concordia Lutheran Seminary is based on books written by professors is beyond shameful and is most certainly sinful. Way to go, Satan!

Readers may, and probably are, saying I am "Lutheran bashing." I think you'll change your mind about that as you read ahead. Remember that I was raised Lutheran. Much of my family is still hanging onto Lutheran roots, as if those might save them. My main goal in this book is to get my own family to read the Bible. They are my first priority. I can do that best by exposing the problems with their indoctrination in the Lutheran Church first and then showing them the indoctrination of others trumpeted in the denominational churches that they attend. It is important to now take a look at those other denominational religions and the pastoral curricula they offer at their seminaries.

While doing research for this book, I investigated the pastoral curricula of various denominational seminaries including: Covenant (Presbyterian) Theological Seminary, the Episcopal Diocese of Rochester, Methodist Theological Center, Most Holy Trinity (Catholic) Seminary, Shawnee Baptist College, and Trinity Lutheran Seminary (ELCA). Due to copyright laws, I am, sadly, unable to publicize the curricula. Before you read any further in this book, however, I would like you to find and thoroughly review the curricula of these seminaries, found at the following Internet Web sites: http://covenantseminary.edu/learn/degreecourseinformation/masterofdivinity/; http://cfte.episcopalrocheter.org/Training/diaconate-training.html; http://www.courseofstudyschoolofohio.com/curriculum/default.html; http://www.mostholytrinityseminary.org/curriculum.html; http://shawneebaptistcollege.org/html/pastoral_theology.html (there is an underline between "pastoral" and "theology"); http://www.trinitylutheranseminary.edu

As you carefully examine each seminary, you will notice that the basic pastoral curriculum taught at each school does not indicate a significant difference from what we just learned is taught at Concordia Lutheran Seminary. All cover church history, theology, preaching, ethics, etc. Some cover music, education, counseling, pastoral care and more. All require a degree of knowledge and competence in Hebrew and Greek. It's important for you to know that I disagree with none of the above requirements. All have a level of necessity in the life of a pastor.

What do I disagree with? Look carefully at the requirement for biblical knowledge. Which of the seminaries require reading, let alone studying, the entire Bible to become an ordained pastor or priest? It should make you and me squirm. I'm certain it pains God's heart. If you haven't read an entire book, how can you teach it? Does anyone recall the Hemingway scenario? Even the study they actually do in the Bible is often limited because only so many things can be covered in a few years. How sad.

I am no expert on the Bible, but the scary fact is that I may know more about that book than many pastors and priests standing in pulpits today. This is simply because I have read and studied the Bible from cover to cover four times; and as we have seen, many pastors and priests haven't read it once—not even once! Yet week after week, people attend various churches and have never considered that fact. Many look at their spiritual shepherd as a type of "god" who is all-knowing. All of us—me included—have believed without question that our pastor or priest has indeed read and studied the Bible from cover to cover. Why would we doubt that? Those who haven't read the entire

Bible believe that their pastor is absolutely the expert in that area when, in reality, very little knowledge of the Bible may separate the pastor or priest from the average person. As one of those average people, it is painful now for me to sit in a church service and hear a pastor present a biblically incorrect statement; but, the good news for God is that I can do that. Can you?

What kind of seminary do you think Jesus would approve of? What message might He give to denominational seminaries and their non-reading of the entire Bible? What did He tell the Pharisees, Sadducees, and Teachers of the Law? What did He think of their "religiosity?" Think about this now: Whom did Jesus personally select to be His teachers and representatives throughout eternity? Whom did He choose to continue His ministry when He ascended into heaven? Did He select a religious leader of any kind? No. Did He require any of them to go to a seminary? No. Was He concerned that none of them were selected by a rabbi as the "best of the best" but were sent home to learn the trades of their fathers? Not at all! Jesus chose ordinary men—fishermen, to be exact—to continue His ministry once He died and ascended to heaven. Those 12 men, along with Paul—a Jew who persecuted Christians—and other people just like you and me, without seminary training, could and did win the world for Christ. If God had wanted pastors trained in a seminary, he would have built one first and then built the church. We all know that is not what He did.

Jesus believed and taught that His Father's book would be sufficient to teach mankind His ways. A pastor once told his congregation that the Bible was written by God for mankind and not by God for Jesus. Jesus knows the Word because He is the Word (John 1:1). If it was, then, written for you and me, why in the world haven't most of us—even the clergy—read it?

Satan has done a great job, hasn't he? He has kept denominational seminaries, pastors, and congregants deceived for more years than any of us would like to count about what is and is not really in the Bible. Again, how is it that pastors have attended seminaries for centuries and never questioned the fact that they weren't required to read the entire Bible? Didn't they ever feel guilty about that? The truth, of course, is that seminaries aren't teachers of the Word but are simply indoctrinators of the religion they represent.

Because of Satan's prowess, Christians are basically ineffective for the Lord; and that ineffectiveness is getting worse, as the Bible predicted it would. Most denominational churches are reaching their own people, but they are not going beyond their own doors, and Satan loves that. Is "internal" witnessing all Jesus asked us to do? Is that the Great Commission? Reality is that people in denominational churches believe they are baptized and confirmed and they're "in"— nothing more is required of them. Witness to someone? Absolutely not!

Bill Weir, weekend anchor of ABC's "Good Morning, America," stated on the air on October 12, 2008: "My grandmother used to tell me never to talk about religion or politics." Satan is thrilled by that proclamation. Mr. Weir's grandmother inadvertently taught him Satan's way, not God's way, and her teaching, and that of many well-meaning people just like her, has a great deal to do with the turning of this nation away from God and to a liberal, tolerant way of thinking. It is an attitude that is pervasive in denominational churches. It's the "let's be nice" theory: Keep Christians nice instead of witnesses for Christ. In reality, it should be through both religion and politics that we govern the world for Christ. That was His original idea, wasn't it?

In effect, most denominational churches have totally thwarted God's plan for the salvation of the world. After all, God saves everyone, doesn't He? Where in the Bible does it say that? What did Jesus say about lukewarm Christians? He said: "I will spew them out of my mouth." He said that it is better to be hot or cold than lukewarm. When you attend your denominational church weekly and never mention the word Jesus again until the next Sunday, are you "hot," "cold," "lukewarm," or simply indifferent. When was the last time you even remotely wondered about, based on your biblical knowledge, a statement your pastor or priest made in his sermon? You don't question because you don't know the Bible well enough to do that. Isn't that right? You can't deny, then, that you are simply a denominational robot, can you?

When was the last time you said to someone, "Lord willing, we'll meet again." Did you know that is a biblical requirement? It is! Just know, though, that you are not alone in your illiteracy, indoctrination, and naivety. Denominational churches are filled weekly with people just like you. I was once one of them. Remember that denominational churches also have wonderful, witnessing Christians in them every Sunday. They are just few and far between.

In four readings of the Bible, I have found no basis for denominational divisions. In fact, the night before Jesus was crucified, He prayed not for the dividing of His people but for the unification of them: "I pray that those who believe in Me through their (the disciples) message ... may be <u>one</u>, Father, just as You are in Me and I am in You ... May they be brought to <u>complete unity</u> to let the world know that You sent Me and have loved them even as You have loved Me." (John 17:20-23). Tell me, folks, where has the denominational church attempted to follow that personal prayer of Jesus? We are not *one*. We can't even commune together as brothers and sisters in Christ. How ridiculous is that?!

In His prayer, Jesus is not asking that we all attend the same church. What He is asking is that as Christians we show *unity* of fellowship and purpose. That is absolutely not happening, nor are denominational churches working toward that goal. In reality, churches are doing all they can to keep Christians divided by doctrine. If churches even made an attempt to at least stand up for the Bible as one in the world, we would be protesting *together* against those things that God detests like abortion, homosexuality, fornication, adultery, etc. Instead, churches write their own Bibles (like the *Book of Concord*), and members won't step into the church of another denomination to save their souls. Amazingly, Christians take that stand all the while believing they are doing what Jesus would have them do. Where did they get that idea?

When will we listen also to Paul as he speaks in I Cor. 1:10-13: "I appeal to you, brothers, in the name of our Lord Jesus Christ, that <u>all of you agree with one another so that there may be no divisions among you and that you may be perfectly united in mind and thought</u>. My brothers, some from Chloe's household have informed me that there are quarrels among you. What I mean is this: One of you says, 'I follow Paul'; another, 'I follow Apollos'; another, 'I follow Cephas'; still another, 'I follow Christ'. Is Christ divided? Was Paul crucified for you? Were you baptized into the name of Paul?" Folks, if Christ's call for unity and Paul's attacks on those who would be divided for the cause doesn't question denominationalism, I don't know what does!

All of us should live by the call of Jesus for unity and the words of I Thessalonians 2:13: "We also thank God continually because when you received the Word of God which you heard from us, you accepted it, <u>not as the word of men</u>, but actually as it is, the Word of God, which is at work in you who believe." Pick up your Bibles, folks, dust them off and read them. Maybe then you'll think twice the next time you drive to your denominational church that doesn't require its leaders to read the Bible from cover to cover and prevents you from worshipping in unity with your brothers and sisters in Christ.

CHAPTER 2

THE ENTRAPMENT OF DENOMINATIONAL CHURCHES

Dr. D. James Kennedy, long-time pastor of Coral Ridge Presbyterian Church in Fort Lauderdale, Florida, and an unending crusader for a Christian America, is one of many Godly men whom I admire. Though he went to heaven a few years ago, his presence is still among us, and his messages can be seen weekly on national television. Dr. Kennedy once told his congregation: "Forty years ago, a professor at a Presbyterian seminary said, 'The day will come when if the Presbyterian Church does not carry out The Great Commission, God will choose someone else to do it.' Dr. Kennedy went on to say, "I believe that is what happened. I believe God chose the Pentecostals. Just think, forty years ago, no one heard of them. Today they have a church everywhere you look."

It's true that while denominational churches are decreasing in large numbers, nondenominational churches are growing in even greater numbers. According to an article entitled "More avoiding denomination labels" in the March 9, 2009, edition of the *Sarasota-Manatee Herald Tribune*: "...the increase in people labeling themselves in more generic Christian terms corresponds with the decline in people identifying themselves as Protestant ... People calling themselves mainline Protestants, including Methodists and Lutherans, have dropped to 13 percent of the population, down from 19 percent in 1990. The number of people who define themselves as generically 'Protestant' went from approximately 17 million in 1990 to 5 million in 2008. Meanwhile, the number of people who use nondenominational terms has gone from 194,000 in 1990 to more than 8 million."[16]

These numbers are staggering and to offset them, mainline churches are doing some research. According to John Adams' article "PCUSA's Reasons for Staggering Loss of Members Aren't Justified by Numbers": "In the year that ended Dec. 31, 2002, a membership loss of 41,812 people (in the Presbyterian Church) was the highest in 20 years." Mr. Adams states that the Presbyterian Church has seen a 37-year decline based on what he believes is the "theological liberalization of the PCUSA." The total membership loss in the 37-year period ending in 2002 accumulated to a staggering 1.8 million. Mr. Adams states that "five mainline sisters (the PCUSA, the United Methodist Church, the Episcopal Church, the United Church of Christ and the Evangelical Lutheran Church) share a lot of baggage on their downward trip." Some of the "baggage" includes the ordination of homosexuals, social tolerance including diversity, and seminaries that do not accept biblical beliefs.[17]

In regards to Presbyterianism, Jack Marcum, head of the Office of Research Services stated the following: "At the rate of membership decline over the last dozen years, we would cease to have any members by the year 2061. The membership of the PCUSA is now less than that of the former United Presbyterian Church USA in 1965. In other words, we have lost the net equivalent of the entire PCUSA membership in just 30 years!" According to author John Adams, "Marcum offered that analysis in 1999. Since then, membership losses have accelerated. Marcum is wrong. There would be no one left—not in 2061—but after 2054."[18]

The Presbyterian Church is not alone in its membership struggles. David Virtue in an article entitled, "Episcopal Church Fights Declining Ordinations, Clergy Loss, Dwindling Membership," writes: "The Episcopal Church faces a triumvirate of problems that is seeing the denomination decimated of people. The church claims 2.4 million members. In reality, less than 800,000 attend weekly services. More than 700 orthodox Episcopalians leave weekly because of the church's rejection of the authority of Scripture and its sub-biblical positions on human sexuality, specifically the blessing of same-sex unions and the consecration of a non-celibate homosexual to the episcopacy. In 2002, 71,000 fewer people attended the Episcopal Church every week and the decline is continuing." According to David Virtue, "the Episcopal Church is the most aging, stagnant denomination in American Protestantism today."[19]

Finally, we take a look at the Catholic Church. In an online article entitled "Why do Catholics Become Evangelicals?" by Gerald Mendoza, we read: "If the growth factor for each country of Latin America is averaged, the Evangelical and Pentecostal percentage of the population there tripled over a period of 25 years.... The same trend is visible in the United States. Many members of Pentecostal and independent charismatic churches are former Catholics."[20]

Mr. Mendoza believes these are some of the reasons Catholics are leaving the church: They don't know their faith well enough to defend it; they don't know their Bibles; and they are unhappy with the lack of preaching and fellowship that brings Evangelicals back to church week after week. Mr. Mendoza claims that "upwards of 100,000 Catholics leave the Church in favor of Evangelical denominations each year. These hundreds of thousands of Evangelical converts have learned or are learning how to evangelize; and they are recruiting their friends, family and co-workers to Protestant Evangelicalism."[21]

Why have mainline churches lost members while evangelical churches are growing by leaps and bounds? Was the Presbyterian seminary professor of 40 years ago right? Is God, who established The Great Commission, blessing those churches that truly follow it? Is The Great Commission being followed because Evangelicals actually read their Bibles in their entirety more than any of those in mainline churches?

In 1873, Charles G. Finney, legendary evangelist of the Great Awakening, said to the pastors of his day, "Brethren, our preaching will bear its legitimate fruits.

If immorality prevails in the land, the fault is ours in a great degree. If the public press lacks moral discrimination, the pulpit is responsible for it. If the church is degenerate and worldly, the pulpit is responsible for it. If the world loses its interest in religion, the pulpit is responsible for it. If Satan rules in our halls of legislation, the pulpit is responsible for it. If our politics become so corrupt that the very foundations of our government are ready to fall away, the pulpit is responsible for it."[22] Though written 136 years ago, these words still ring true today—eerily true.

The church has acquiesced to the liberalization of society. We accept everything and anything because Satan has duped us into believing his lies, and he has been successful because mankind is more into the world than into the Word. I believe that not knowing the Word and, therefore, not being able to defend it may be one of the world's greatest sins.

While mainline Protestant churches are declining, Evangelical Protestant churches are growing, "stealing" parishioners, and building mega churches. Saddleback Church begun by Pastor Rick Warren has more than 12 million members. Joel Osteen's Lakewood Church in Houston has over 35,000 members. I believe these churches are flourishing because people are beginning to see the indoctrination of the church versus the pure truth of the Word. God is alive and well and lets us know that in the pages of Scripture. He tells us what has been, what is, and what is to come. Only those who have read the entire Bible will see His plan for the future—the final stages of which, I believe, are being played out right now.

While I would never again join a mainline church (even though there are some that do preach the entire Bible and are fully committed to Christ), I think it is important to stress here that not all nondenominational churches preach the pure Word either. Be very careful what church you join. What looks good isn't always good. How will you, if you are biblically illiterate, however, discern the difference?

On April 7, 2009, I changed television channels when I came across Joel Osteen and his wife on the "Larry King Live" show. I don't watch Pastor Osteen very often because what I have seen hasn't impressed me. I know that will rile some of his most ardent supporters, but I was even more convinced I was right about the Osteens as I listened to their April interview.

Larry King asked Joel Osteen who wrote the Bible. This is Pastor Osteen's answer: "It was written by different men like you and me, but I *believe* it was inspired by the Holy Spirit." What Pastor Osteen "believes" should be unimportant to people. What needed to be said is that all Scripture is *God-breathed,* and it should have been explained that Paul wrote those words. It is important in these perilous times that pastors stop talking about "us" and our "beliefs" but, rather, quote Scripture. For a pastor to do anything less on national television makes me very skeptical. I feel Joel Osteen badly missed the mark here.

Larry King then asked Mrs. Osteen to comment. She said: "I was raised in a Christian home. I was raised believing that." What kind of an answer is that to a dying world? Some so-called Christian homes teach that homosexuals were born homosexual. That doesn't make that home correct—certainly not biblically correct. Though the teachings of a true Christian home are priceless, all that really matters is what the Bible says. In this interview, Mrs. Osteen gave more credence to her Christian upbringing than to her God.

Please don't misunderstand me here. I have great respect for my Christian parents and my Christian upbringing, but I need to answer mankind with wisdom from the Bible and not wisdom from my wonderful home. Mrs. Osteen should have been better prepared for the interview. After all, she and her husband pastor a church with a weekly attendance, according to their Web site, of approximately 47,000 people and minister on television to many more than that. Larry King went on to say to Mrs. Osteen: "It makes you feel good." She replied, "Yes, it makes me feel good." Drugs make people feel good, too! What a poor answer in defense of such a great God! True religion has nothing to do with "feeling good" and everything to do with honoring God in everything we say and do.

I expected more of the Osteens on national television, and I believe those who support them should expect more of them, too. I know God expected more of them. They were given an incredible opportunity to witness, and they gave, at best, lukewarm answers. That interview did make me question just how biblically literate they really are. Having said that, it is also important for us to understand that Joel Osteen and his wife are human and have human failings. I just hope that they are better prepared to speak for Jesus next time.

I'd also like to speak about Pastor Rick Warren. He impressed me when he interviewed both Senators John McCain and Barack Obama just prior to the November 2008 elections. Clearly, Pastor Warren had prepared well for those interviews. I'm sure his followers will be unhappy, however, when they now read that I very much disliked his book *The Purpose Driven Life*. The Holy Spirit riled my spirit as I read that book, and I never finished it. I realize that it sold millions of copies, but that doesn't impress me. I believe to this day that there is something very unbiblical in that book—more New Age than Scriptural, in my opinion. My church asked if I would serve as a home group leader to discuss the book. I told them that I could not do that because I didn't believe the book was Scriptural. There have been many critiques written about the book. One of the best I found was a pamphlet written by Dr. Noah Hutchings of Southwest Radio Ministries.

My point is that large churches run by charismatic leaders do not always preach the pure Word of God. To be fair, I have never been to Saddleback Church nor have I ever heard Pastor Warren preach. I am, however, skeptical of the words in his book.

Be discerning about the church you join. Be certain it is biblically based before supporting it. Just because a church makes you "feel good" doesn't mean it is biblically sound, and the latter is all that matters. Be absolutely certain that your pastor has read the Bible from cover to cover and expects you to do the same. Two people cannot be on the same wavelength unless they have both read the book that establishes that wavelength. If you have a biblical question, make sure it's discussed with an open Bible and not a denominational book. Accept nothing less than God as the head of your church, and be certain that the Bible is taught in its entirety and its truth, not in some manmade doctrine. There is only one way you'll know that—read the Word!

CHAPTER 3

STUDY YOUR BIBLE, PREPARE FOR YOUR FINALS:

BIBLE—*B*asic *I*nstructions *B*efore *L*eaving *E*arth

Just as Satan is having a field day with seminaries at denominational churches, He is also having a field day with those who sit in the pews every week. You and I—not the pastors, priests, or churches—are responsible for what pew we choose to sit in. God will one day hold the church responsible for its failings, but He'll also hold you and me responsible for ours. How much thought have you really given to the church you attend?

It is Sunday morning and you are, I hope, about to drive off to your church. For most of you, it's the denomination you have attended for a lifetime. I want this Sunday morning to be different for you, though. At the end of the service, I want you to ask yourself this question: "What is the real reason I'm going to this particular church?" and be honest—brutally honest. Think long and hard before you answer. If your answer is anything but "I am going to this church because I learn something new every week; I am being led to read and study the Bible from cover to cover; and I'm developing a personal relationship weekly with Christ," drive home and tell yourself that you will never again return to that church. As tough as it may be, stick to it! Pray hard and ask God where *He* wants you to attend. The road to a new church is a difficult one. You may have to let go of all the things that made you comfortable in your old church—family, friends, a social life you loved, the committees on which you served, heritage, tradition, etc. As a result, you may even be ridiculed by people you dearly love. None of that will matter, though, the day God calls you home. What will matter is did you answer *His* call; did you read and study *His* Word; and have you grown in grace and in the knowledge of your Lord and Savior Jesus Christ?

What is the result of sitting in a pew week after week with little knowledge of the Bible? What does that do to your Christian walk through life and your church's teaching? I'd like you to consider five consequences of your choice, and that of your church, not to read and study the entire Bible:

1. Biblical illiteracy leads to "the Bible according to (insert your name your here)." Since you don't have a clue what is really in the Book, or you know only what you have been taught on Sundays, you simply write in your mind what you *think* or *hope* the Bible says

or does not say. You use the Bible *you* wrote to make excuses for the behavior of others. God becomes "the god of make believe." People like to make up their own truths because life is more comfortable that way. You can, in your mind, make God anything you want Him (or for some people, her) to be. You can, and probably do, excuse those who sin. Instead of calling sin what it is—sin—you don't say anything. You are quiet when people choose to live together out of wedlock, even though the Bible says that it's absolutely not acceptable in the eyes of God. You can accept abortion even if you wouldn't abort a baby yourself. Yet, all the while you are being tolerant, children created by God—as part of His plan for His kingdom—are losing their right to life. And very few Christians are doing anything about it.

Biblical illiteracy allows you to be a Sunday Christian because you are baptized, confirmed, and saved, even though Jesus' brother James tells us that "faith without works is dead." Where are your works that prove your faith? You can have a "live and let live" mentality, which gives you an excuse not to witness, but James also says, "You adulterous people, don't you know that friendship with the world is hatred toward God? Anyone who chooses to be a friend of the world becomes an enemy of God." The "bible" you have written for yourself may give you peace and keep you from being challenged, but has it also made you an enemy of God without your even realizing it? How is *your* bible working for you? How many people have been saved by the words of God through you and *your* bible?

To my amazement, I hear Christians say, "The Bible is outdated." That shows how uninformed

Christians really are. Clearly, the Bible has never been more relevant. A pastor once said that the whole purpose of the Bible is to see Jesus come and to see Him come again. I definitely know that unless Christians read the entire Bible, they will be like the Israelites who were so involved in Jewish tradition that they missed the Savior despite all the information about His coming available to them in Scripture. Likewise, many Christians who attend church every Sunday will undoubtedly miss the second coming—and perhaps even the rapture that precedes it—because they were steeped in church tradition—Satan's tool—rather than in the words of the Bible.

Jesus tells us that with the right information, we will not know the day or the hour of His coming again, but we will know the season. He sets up a clear picture of that for us throughout both the Old and the New Testaments but especially in Revelation. The events we read about every day in the newspaper are found in the Bible. Those of us who know what the Bible teaches have the ability to follow the steps that Jesus laid out for us to follow. Though the rapture will occur, Jesus will not return until there is peace in Israel, the Antichrist sets up his worship in the temple, and we are a cashless society, etc. Churches that don't teach this fall directly into Satan's hands, and when Satan sends the Antichrist, even Christians will fall for his rhetoric. Will our churches be held accountable for that, along with those of us who chose to ignore the Bible that has collected dust on coffee tables? I believe the answer to that is a definite "yes!"

I also hear Christians say: "The Bible, written by men, has been changed over the years. We can't believe a book like that." Paul tells us that "all Scripture is God-breathed." Peter tells us in 2 Peter 1:16-20: "We did not follow cleverly invented stories when we told you about the power and coming of our Lord Jesus Christ, but we were eyewitnesses to His majesty. For He received honor and glory from God the Father when the voice came to him from the Majestic Glory saying, 'This is my Son, whom I love; with Him I am well pleased.' We ourselves heard this voice that came from heaven when we were with Him on the sacred mountain.... Above all, you must understand that no prophecy of Scripture came about by the prophet's own interpretation. For prophecy never had its origin in the will of man, but men spoke from God as they were carried along by the Holy Spirit." All of the disciples had firsthand knowledge of Jesus, and, in the end, they died horrific deaths for the faith they had in Him. No earthly men would give up their lives in such horrendous ways unless they truly believed what they saw and heard. No man wrote the Bible. The Holy Spirit did. He wrote the Bible for all eternity. It doesn't change because God doesn't change. God says that in His Word.

The disciples also had a historian who carried their work to the people. A man by the name of Josephus wrote about the events of the New Testament and confirmed what the Bible had said. According to The History Channel, there is more manuscript support for the New Testament than for any other body of ancient literature. Over 5,000 Greek and 8,000 Latin manuscripts, as well as many manuscripts in other languages, attest to the integrity of the New Testament. The great majority of existing manuscripts are in substantial agreement. Even though many are late and none are earlier than the 5th century, most of their readings are verified by ancient papyri, ancient versions and quotations of the early church.

In regards to the Old Testament, 2,000-year-old scrolls called the Dead Sea Scrolls were found by a young boy in the late 1940s in caves near the Dead Sea east of Jerusalem. Those scrolls contain the earliest known copies of every book of the Hebrew Bible except the book of Esther, as well as apocryphal texts and descriptions of rituals of a Jewish sect at the time of Jesus. The texts on papyrus date from the third century B.C. to the first century A.D.[23]

The Bible is real and relevant. Why haven't you read it rather than writing your own or listening to the one written by your denomination?

2. Biblical illiteracy has led to a denominational monopoly. Pastors and priests believe their church is the only right church, and they never question seminaries that don't teach the Bible in its entirety. Congregants don't question it, either. Denominational churches thrive because God's people remain ignorant of His Word. As long as people read half—or less—of the Bible, denominations will never die. If all of God's people read and studied the Bible in its entirety with only the Holy Spirit as their guide, the doors of many, many churches may be permanently closed, as I believe they should be. Jesus said in Matthew 22:29: "You are

in error because you do not know the Scriptures nor the power of God." Luke 24:45 says, "Then He opened their minds so they could understand the Scriptures."

Is it possible that God hasn't opened your mind because you haven't been interested? You've allowed a pastor or priest, seminary or church to be your Bible guide even though you now know that many don't teach—or even know—the entire Bible. You have a mind closed to God through the ignorance and lack of knowledge of supposedly learned men. How does Jesus feel about this? In Matthew 15:6-9, He says, "You nullify the word of God for the sake of your tradition. You hypocrites! Isaiah was right when he prophesied about you (Isaiah 29:13): These people honor me with their lips but their hearts are far from me. They worship me in vain; their teachings are but rules taught by men." And you thought Jesus was only talking to the Jews, right? Think again!

People who believe without checking do not walk in truth but in blindness and pass that blindness along to others. Take another look at your church. The Devil, as the great deceiver, has influenced the church. Who wrote the rules—God or man? How would you know? The rules, wisdom, and unfailing love of God are in the Bible. If you haven't read it, you don't know the rules. You only know the ones your church teaches you.

3. Biblical illiteracy leads to a life of manmade rules. What are these manmade "rules" that you live by and would die for? Let's take a look at them. Does your church make you feel guilty if you don't follow the rules of men? For instance, if your church has

Wednesday night services and you don't go, are you made to feel guilty? Please show me in the Bible where it says Wednesday night services are required? If your church has Advent and Lenten services and you don't go, do you feel guilty? If your church says you can't eat meat on Friday and you do, is that a sin? Where in the Bible does it require that? More importantly, why didn't you question a change in that thinking when the church decided that eating meat on Friday really wasn't a sin any more? Since when does sin lose its "sinfulness"? This would have been the moment I went in search of a new church. Why haven't you? If you had read your Bible, you very well might have left your church. If your church tells you that you don't have a voice in the church because it is an elder-run church, why have you accepted that? The Bible says that *all* men and women have been given gifts and *all* are members of the same body. *All* of the gifts come together to make the church what it is. If your pastor says, "By the authority given me as a called and ordained servant of the Word, I now forgive you all of your sins," why do you believe he has the power to do that? According to the Bible, Jesus gave that power only to the apostles. I found nowhere in the Word where that power was passed along to pastors or priests. The only one who can forgive your sins is God. Earthly man—whether or not he has the title of pastor or priest—cannot forgive sins. Nothing in the Bible gives man the authority to do that—nothing!

Where is there support in the Bible for "close" or "closed" communion (believe me when I say that "close" communion really does mean "closed")? Paul tells us in Corinthians that man is to "examine

<u>himself</u>." No where does it give that authority to a pastor or priest. It is true that man can eat and drink the communion elements to his or her damnation (and churches fail in their duty when they don't mention this before serving communion), but the examination of that is not up to anyone but man himself. Why have you as members of a "closed" or "close" church accepted false teaching all these years? Communion's purpose is to "proclaim the Lord's death until He comes." Some churches tell me that I can't commune with Christians in other denominations. The Bible says that nowhere. I can commune with any Christian in any church—or anywhere else, for that matter—as long as I have examined myself. Communion is simply a public gathering of proclamation. It tells others that Jesus is real and will return. You—and I—have believed a myth rather than the truth of the Word.

Perhaps the biggest fault is with Baptist churches that teach (and not all of them do) that the only real Bible is the King James Version. Worst of all, if the church says it, people believe it without investigation. Again, where in the Bible does it say the only valid version belongs to King James?

I believe the most important consideration in Bible reading is not what Bible you read because the Holy Spirit can and does work through any Bible. What I feel is most important is that everyone—and I do mean everyone—reads and studies some version of the Bible from cover to cover. Not everyone is a good reader. Not everyone can take the language of the King James Bible and make sense of it. Many would-be Bible readers would simply give up Bible reading all together if the only Bible they were allowed to read were the King James Version. To my Baptist friends who advocate only the King James Version, rather than condemn someone for not reading it, perhaps we would all be better off if we managed to get everyone to read some Bible—any Bible—that they can understand. The real question here is: What would Jesus do?

It's time we are realistic about people. God didn't give all of us the skills needed to read and understand the King James Version, whose words were written for the people of that time. We don't live in that time nor do we use that language. Just read the version that you feel comfortable with, and let the Holy Spirit do the rest. Why would we place—and insist on—a King James Version above the ability of the Holy Spirit to teach us what is right?

4. Biblical illiteracy leads to tolerance that is unbiblical. People who have not read the Bible are beginning to accept everything people do as okay, including religions that do not lead to Jesus. There was a story written by Gregg Krupa in *The Detroit News* entitled "Interfaith Book Shatters Barriers, Fosters Dialogue." A book called, *The Faith Club,* was written by three women of different faiths. The book discusses the similarities between Judaism, Islam, and Christianity and, hopefully, builds bridges. The idea of this book is a good one—living together in peace with those who believe things differently from us.[24] I have no problem with that. A peaceful, friendly relationship is a great beginning; but that's all it is—a beginning! The Bible requires much more of us than that. God says,

"To whom much is given, much is expected." God's purpose for us on this earth is to witness and not simply to tolerate. Tolerance makes life easier, but it thwarts God's plan to "make disciples of all nations." It is important to remember the real reason that God placed us here—to witness. Though we are to be kind to all, we are not to be tolerant of things that are unGodly, and, above all, we are to let others know that the only way to heaven is through faith in Jesus Christ. Don't forget that though the God of Judaism and the God of Christianity are the same, Allah of Islam is not. I already proved that earlier in the book.

5. Finally, biblical illiteracy has led to ineffective Christianity. We are to be Christians first and church members second. If we lived by that philosophy, just think what we could do on earth for the Lord. We could together fight all things unGodly. But, we choose to "live and let live." We go to our churches on Sunday and back into the world on Monday trying not to offend anyone. Is that what the Bible tells us to do? Why can't we get beyond this? Because we are (you put your religion here) first and, heaven forbid, we would never step into another church for any reason. We can't even come together to support a Godly cause unless our own church supports it.

I think we feel that God personally built the denominational church to which we belong and absolutely did not build the churches of our friends and neighbors. In reality, we Christians simply haven't done the jobs God gave us to do because we are tied to our churches and their manmade doctrines more than we are tied to our

Bibles. I believe Christians bear the brunt for many of the things we abhor in the world today. We sat quietly in our pews while Satan took over our world. The truth is that our Sunday duty to our churches allowed the anti-God, anti-morality, anti-Bible, anti-values attitudes to prevail in our world. There is no reason that we can't go to our own churches on Sunday but work together as Christians in the world Monday through Saturday.

A letter written by Pastor Daniel Johnson of the Evangelical Covenant Church discusses Christians' lack of witnessing and the churches' responsibility for this: "It seems that much, if not most, of 'ministry' is about keeping everything going inside the church... I have been struggling more and more to see how all of this activity and focus and priority line up with Jesus' intentions and expectations for his church when he said, 'Go and make disciples,' not 'Stay and maintain an institution or organization...'"[25]

One of the primary reasons Christians are not witnessing is because we have taken the easy and safe way out of doing so by hiding within and behind our churches. They're not witnessing so why should we. They are committing funds to missions—a very good thing—but have missed the "missions" in their own backyards because they are too busy internally. Since our churches don't remind us of the Great Commission and our responsibility to it, we don't feel compelled to speak about Jesus outside of our church walls. After all, we might offend someone or be personally ridiculed. Yet, the Great Commission is the main reason we're here. It's why God sent the Holy Spirit to us. To that end, I commend the Baptists who are evangelizing the neighborhoods. How about the rest of us? We go to church every week and participate in functions in the church, but when it comes to witnessing, we do little or nothing. That keeps us safe, but it also makes us ineffective and non-functioning for Jesus. We're doing a great job down here on earth, aren't we? We read our Bibles very little, if at all, and we fail to witness. I wonder how God feels about that.

Just think of all the things you have missed because you haven't read the Bible. I hope you are now seeing who owns the responsibility for biblical illiteracy in our world—the church and you. The church is biblically illiterate because even its leaders haven't read the entire Bible. You are biblically illiterate because you made a choice not to read the entire Bible. Because of this, you have written your own Bible truths. You have allowed biblically illiterate denominations to flourish. You have accepted Bible rules made by man because you think church leaders know more than you. You have been tolerant of things God abhors, and you and millions of others who call themselves Christians have become completely ineffective in the world, standing up for God rarely—if at all.

When will you begin to do the things God expects? First, you have to meet Him personally and know just what He expects, and the only place those expectations are found is in His Word. Just how far are you in reading that entire Word? You will be amazed at the joy you will experience when you finally do what God says. Your whole life will change. That change will change the lives of others, too. That's the idea of the cross—to save you, me and others. Let's carry that cross and its message everywhere—the message of the Bible that you—and for many years, I—forgot to read.

CHAPTER 4

IT'S ALL ABOUT TOMORROW

When our children were 13, 11 and 8, my husband and I took them to see the stage production of "Annie." For whatever reason, our youngest son was captivated by that play—so much so, in fact, that when he learned it would be presented at his high school, he tried out for it and was given a part. A favorite song in that play begins "The sun will come out tomorrow." The song represents real hope in the lives of young girls who have only known the loneliness of an orphanage. Hope keeps people going even when the going gets mighty tough.

If you think about it, all of us are seeking hope in a world where we don't belong and a world where we will live but a brief time. Life seems as if it will go on forever, and that's especially true when we are young. But if you take but a moment to review history, you quickly realize just how brief life really is. Look around you. The vast majority of everyone you see will be gone from this earth in 100 years. No one has stayed here and no one ever will, though we who are saved will come back with Jesus on the day that He returns. That is biblical.

Those of us who have lived beyond age 60 certainly begin to see the truth of our mortality. It is then that we realize that for us as Christians, "Annie" had it all wrong. What will actually happen tomorrow is that, according to the Bible, the sun will, one day soon, not come out but will be darkened, and the moon will turn to blood. The real truth of the Bible, however, is that "the **Son** will come some tomorrow," and I personally believe the beginning of that "tomorrow" has already occurred.

Because I have read the entire Bible, I eagerly read about that "tomorrow" every day in the newspaper. As Orphan Annie knew in her hopes and dreams, life is not about today. It truly is about "tomorrow." If you know what the Bible says, not only will "tomorrow" not surprise you, but you'll be prepared and will be looking forward to it. Watching God's plan for His people unfold—a plan that has my name on it—is amazing, and I found it all in His Word, just as you will if you open it as well as read and study it all.

Previous generations should have read the Bible rather than rely on the church to do that for them. Since they didn't live in the last days—as I believe we are—they didn't necessarily need knowledge of the signs of the end. Yet, by not reading the Bible, they chose to spend eternity, if they were saved, with a God they really didn't know. They chose to know Him only through the eyes of others.

Spiritual death is manifesting itself all over America and throughout the world. The Gospel has been watered down. Church has become a ritual and an obligation—a place of comfort where our heritage can be lived out and where people of the same cultural background can find a "comfort zone"—a familiarity. Bibles sit on coffee tables unread, and seminaries produce doctrinal robots rather than Bible-literate shepherds for Christ. Paul said in Ephesians 1:9-10: "And He (God) made known to us (through His Word) the mystery of His will according to His good pleasure, which He purposed in Christ, to be put into effect when the times will have reached their fulfillment—to bring all things in heaven and on earth under one head, even Christ." I see the signs of that "bringing" and that "fulfillment." The Bible's words in the second to the last verse of the entire book are: "Amen. Come Lord Jesus." I believe He's coming soon, and I also say, "Come, Lord Jesus." How ready are you to meet the Lord? When He asks you what books you read down there, what will your answer be?

My urgency in getting you to read the whole Bible has to do with Jesus' coming again. I have long believed that I was meant to write this book. Interestingly though, until now, I simply couldn't find the time to do it. As I look back over that scenario, I see clearly that this book had to be written in God's time, not mine. I believe the economic and spiritual downfall of America makes the timing of this book perfect. God knew all about that, and I pray you will heed my warning to read and study the Bible and examine your faith, your church, and your witness. Are you spiritually dead or leaning in that direction without realizing it? Are you "church-doctrine rich" and "Bible poor"? Have you defended your church and its beliefs more than you've defended the Word? Do you know enough about the Bible to defend it at all? You may think so; but when you read and study it all, you may be just as surprised as I was at how little you really know. If Jesus came today, will He speak to you these words found in Revelation: "Well done, thou good and faithful servant?" How many people are going to heaven because of your witness?

Perhaps there should be more in your warehouse and less in your showroom. Going to church on Sunday produces a good "showroom" in the eyes of your community, but building a warehouse of information from God's Word makes you an effective witness for Him and allows you to carry out the Great Commission. It allows you to know if your pastor is speaking God's Word. It shows you how to live God's way rather than the way you *think* God would have us live. Is your life a showroom or a warehouse? Many thanks to Stan Pavkovich, pastor of Church of the Cross in Bradenton, Florida, for making this important distinction come alive for me.

God disciplines nations that turn away from Him. Look around you. Do you see any of those? How about Europe? Is it America's turn? Is America spiritually dead, or is it busy dying slowly and digging its grave to that end? What have you and I contributed to that? Christians of all denominations as well as those who are nondenominational, we desperately need to work together to bring the world back to God and away from its present path of spiritual death.

Over thousands of years, God, in His Word, has told you and me and all those He created and will create that He will rapture His people and then return to earth one day with them to conquer evil forever and establish His eternal kingdom among men. My church had it wrong. There is now, however, no excuse for placing our faith more in seminaries than in the Word. John 17:17 says, "Sanctify them through your truth; your Word is truth." That truth will set us free, just as God said it would. If you got to the end of this book, you just may be on your way to that wonderful freedom that only the Holy Spirit can give—freedom from the denominational chains that bind mankind.

I'm not asking you to believe or accept one thing I have written in this book. I'm only asking that what I've written here leads you to read the Bible on your own to prove me wrong. Remember, though, you have to read it from cover to cover leaving your denominational bias behind you.

Changing a pattern or habit isn't easy, but it's always worth it. My prayer is that you make an immediate, prayerful decision to read and study the Bible in its entirety, as I believe time is running out for mankind. The Bible is not a "give me, book." It takes time, effort and energy to get through it; but it is so worth all of that. As you read it, read the daily newspaper along with it. It won't be long before you'll see God's plan coming alive, just as my husband and I have seen. May God truly bless your journey through His Word. What an incredible journey it will be!

If you have read this book but have never accepted Christ as your Savior, I urge you to do so right now. Isaiah 55:6,7 says: "Seek the Lord <u>while you can find him</u>. Call on him <u>now while he is near</u>...Yes, turn to our God, for he will abundantly pardon." Isaiah tells us that God will not always be there for us to be saved. There will be an end to His salvation invitation. When will that end be? No one knows, so there is an urgency to call on Him now.

The first step in salvation is easy. Simply ask Jesus to come into your heart, forgive all of your sins, and take over your life from this day forward. Then let Him lead you and make life's decisions for you. (If you're anything like me, you haven't been doing such a good job making those decisions on your own anyway, have you?) Jesus is waiting to hear from you. Once you commit your life to Him, make it a priority to read the Bible from cover to cover. Remember that accepting Christ is only a first step. It is a beginning, not an end. God doesn't offer "cheap grace." I am reminded of the title of a wonderful Gospel song, "When He was on the cross, I was on His mind." Jesus took a punishment that He didn't deserve to save us eternally. We should be so thankful that we want to give Him a "healthy return on His investment."

Once saved, Jesus does not expect us to bask in the laurels of that moment. The release from the burdens of sin and a promise of eternity with Jesus bring about powerful changes in our lives and provide us with incredible peace. As saved brothers and sisters in Christ, Jesus expects us to learn all we can about Him and to grow in our faith. We are to be publicly baptized as believers, not as infants, to affirm our faith. Jesus said, "If you do not acknowledge me publicly, I will not acknowledge you before my Father who is in Heaven." Jesus is our intercessor in heaven. We cannot be saved except by Him. God the Father accepts us because when He looks at us, He sees His Son. Jesus said, "No one comes to the Father but by Me."

If you have just asked Jesus into your heart, welcome to the family of God! Now, get to work. Find a place to worship where God is honored—a place free of denominational biases and where the Bible is taught in its truth and in its entirety. Find a place where you are encouraged to read God's Word from cover to cover, where witnessing is a priority, and where you can grow in grace. Be God's earthly witness and not just the church's servant. Reject the notion of "cheap grace." Thank Jesus for what He did for you by serving Him daily. I definitely look forward to meeting you in heaven if I don't meet you first on earth.

In regards to witnessing for and devoting one's life to Christ, here is a story all of us should ponder. A young Lutheran pastor by the name of Dietrich Bonhoeffer served God in an amazing way in Hitler's Nazi Germany. In September of 1938, he and a Jewish friend left the underground seminary begun for their protection in the village of Finkenwalde. Bonhoeffer had become "bitterly disappointed by the leaders of the Confessing Church who had remained silent when most of its pastors had sworn an oath to Adolph Hitler... (Are you gasping at this? The clergy did this so they could get money for their churches. Such money came from people's taxes and was distributed by the government.)

In Bonhoeffer's Europe, God had increasingly been moved to the margins of social, political, and even religious life. In (his book) *The Cost of Discipleship*, Bonhoeffer complained that <u>the German church was offering 'cheap grace,' a cut-rate gospel that required little of believers</u>."[26] Does anyone see America here? Prior to this, we haven't heard much about those lukewarm, Hitler-supporting churches, have we? I wonder why, don't you?

On Fox News' "Huckabee" program, May 29, 2010, Eric Metaxas, author of *Bonhoeffer*, stated that Pastor Bonhoeffer tried to get the churches to understand that their faith required them to fight against the Nazi regime. God would want them to do just that. When nothing he tried worked, he joined the German military intelligence so he could reach the Allies and inform them of what was going on in his country. He also became a spy and was part of a plot to kill Hitler.

Pastor Bonhoeffer, engaged to be married, was captured and later hung by the Nazis in 1945, just weeks before the liberation of Germany. He had stood against evil and had served God to the very end of his life, not swearing an oath to Hitler as his fellow pastors had done. Bonhoeffer was not seeking "cheap grace" from God nor did he consider his life more important than his witness. He did exactly what God expects of us. He stood up for Jesus, even knowing that death could very well be the result.

Just think—we probably never would have heard of Dietrich Bonhoeffer had he, like his fellow pastors, taken an oath to Hitler. By the way, can you name any of those pastors? God had a plan for Pastor

Bonhoeffer's life, and Bonhoeffer obeyed. That is the cost of discipleship—Jesus first. "Cheap grace" is simply not part of the package. We aren't saved by our works; but without them, our faith is dead. I wonder whatever happened to those pastors who swore allegiance to Hitler, moved God to the fringes, and offered cheap grace.

America is dying spiritually, more and more every day. The American church is often into itself, and so are its members. Sin is no longer considered sin; tolerance prevails in the name of Jesus. It is a tolerance, by the way, that Jesus abhors. In America today, the Bible— even among some Christians and their churches— is simply a book to be challenged or dusted from time to time, not read, believed, and lived by. If anyone doubts that Christ is coming soon, they have simply missed the warnings. They are in darkness. Biblical illiteracy is clearing the way to America's eventual spiritual death.

I hope one day the prayer of Jesus in Gethsemane will be answered: "...that all of them may be <u>one</u> as we are one—I in them and you in me. May they be brought to <u>complete unity</u> to let the world know that you sent me and have loved them even as you have loved Me. Father, I want those you have given Me to be with Me where I am." Let's get busy and know our Bibles well enough to pass the message of God's love and forgiveness on to others. Lord, use the literacy of your Word to tear down the walls of denominational deception and blind indoctrination, whether innocent or not. Open our eyes to your truth, and move us to live for you each and every day of our lives.

I leave you with these words of God written in Acts 20:32: "And now I (Paul, and Gail, too) entrust you to God and the word of His grace—<u>His message</u> that is able to build you up and give you an inheritance with all those He has set apart for Himself."

"I look forward to the day when we stop serving a denomination and start serving God."

John Hagee, Pastor
Cornerstone Church
San Antonio, Texas
November 14, 2009

EPILOGUE

Y̶ou are now aware that spiritual blindness, due in large part to biblical illiteracy, rules Europe today and is clearly invading America. The Bible says this will be true just before Jesus returns. We are told that the world will be as it was in Noah's day, and in that day, only eight people were saved—just eight.

America's fall began, I believe, in the 1960s. Daily newspapers and television broadcasts bring the sins of Noah's day to light every day to those of us the Bible has enlightened. That was never clearer than the college reunion I attended on March 3, 2010. It painted for me a present-day picture of America now being played out on the campus of a Christian liberal arts college that I attended for two years in Ohio.

Capital University held its annual alumni gathering in several locations in Florida, including the city in which my husband and I spend the winter. I attended two of those meetings—a luncheon at the home of a Capital graduate and a dinner at a beautiful country club. Four people were present directly from Capital— the president, vice-president, alumni coordinator, and a professor of education. At the luncheon meeting, Capital's president shared with alumni that $46 million was recently raised in a campaign, and Capital had several faculty members recognized for their excellence. Its 625 freshmen came to the campus with the highest GPA in Capital's history, and 25 of them were valedictorians of their high schools. That class also registered the highest ACT scores since records were kept at the university. On the outside, in the "showroom," it appears Capital is doing well. As the gathering progressed, President Denvy Bowman, who has done an amazing job turning around Capital's once horrendous financial burdens, then entertained questions from the audience. Interestingly, the majority of those questions centered around religious education on campus.

Capital was founded in 1830 by German Lutheran immigrants and was built for the sole purpose of honoring and teaching Jesus Christ to its students during the educational process and preparing some for the pastoral and teaching ministry. As a student there in the 1960s, chapel was required three times a week, and religious classes were also required. Sunday attendance at Christ Lutheran Church across the street from the campus was a "given."

Alumni in attendance at the reunion had experienced the same religious training at Capital that I received. They were clearly concerned about the religious changes they had heard about and had seen there. The president did an excellent job of trying to be as honest as he felt he could be. He was fully aware of his audience. He admitted that presently only 17 percent of the student body is Lutheran, up from a previous 13 percent (though the majority of students were Lutheran when I attended there). He further explained that there is a change in the relationship between the college and the seminary. Once an integral part of the college, the seminary now carries on a cordial relationship with the college but is a separate entity. The president related that when a nearby Episcopal seminary closed, its students were admitted to Capital's seminary (now called Trinity Lutheran Seminary), while keeping their Episcopalian identity. The faces of the attendees displayed their wonderment at that idea.

Perhaps the most revealing picture of spiritual blindness came from a pastor's wife in attendance. She was raised in Detroit. Since that is at the heart of my childhood roots, I asked her where in the city she was from. I learned that her childhood home was very near mine, and she actually attended elementary school with my brother and sister. We then exchanged information about our backgrounds. She proceeded to tell me that she had lived in Florida many years, and her husband had started a Lutheran Church there. She explained that Lutheran churches are struggling now due to the hierarchy's acceptance of homosexuality. She then said she couldn't understand why members were having difficulty with this since homosexuals were obviously created that way. I politely replied that I didn't believe that and that it doesn't matter what we personally believe but only what the Bible says. I said that the Bible is clear that homosexuality is wrong. She then said, "Jesus never said it was wrong." I said, "Yes, He very definitely did." She said, "You'll have to show me that." Believing this was neither the time nor the place to further discuss the issue, I simply told her I'd be glad to do that.

What, you may ask, is the problem here? The problem is that this is a pastor's wife who is not only unaware of biblical truths but lacks an understanding of who Jesus really is. Worst of all, she is proclaiming biblical untruths to the world, including her church. The fact is that God Himself called homosexuality an abomination in more than one place in the Bible and destroyed the cities of Sodom and Gomorrah because of that and many other sins. An even greater fact is that Jesus **is** God! Jesus said in John 10:30: "I and the Father are one." The Bible creates a clear picture of a trinity for us—Father, Son and Holy Spirit—one God, not three. Jesus absolutely did say that homosexuality is an abomination because He is God and God is Jesus. Obviously, spiritual blindness has so invaded the Lutheran Church that even a pastor's wife, without hesitation, publicly proclaims that which is not biblically accurate. The membership role of the Lutheran Church is rapidly declining. Is it possible that God has taken His Hand of blessing off of a religion that does not now claim Bible truths?

The evening gathering of Capital alumni was even more eye-opening. Alumni again questioned what they perceive as a lack of religious training at a once proud Lutheran college. Again, the president stated that only 17 percent of the college is Lutheran, but this time, he went on to discuss the dichotomy of the student population. He proudly announced that there are more Catholics on campus than enrollment in the Catholic college in the area. He said there is a large Jewish population on campus, as well as Muslim students. He let the alumni know just how important diversity is—so much so that Capital today recognizes Ramadan as a viable holiday to be observed on campus. I sat there stunned. Ramadan, a Muslim holiday, is being respected at a Lutheran college! How did that come to be? Something is very wrong with that statement. Where is the outpouring of anger in that regard from the alumni?

Sadly, hypocrisy obviously runs rampant at Capital, and it's time alumni, parents, students, and church leaders recognize what is going on there. Diversity at a historically Lutheran university is hypocritical. The God of Lutheranism is not the Allah of Ramadan. Jesus who died on the cross and through whom Lutherans have always claimed salvation is not the Messiah the Jews are waiting for but the One who has already come. Dedicated German Lutherans who gave their all to establish and maintain Capital University would feel betrayed if they could see Capital today. It certainly is not the Capital I once knew.

It's time Capital says to the world, "We are no longer a Lutheran university but simply an excellent liberal arts school in the state of Ohio, with fine academic programs in the fields of business, law, music, and others (all of which is true)." God has asked us not to be a friend to the world but witnesses for Him. The Capital of today is, I believe, dishonoring the God of the Bible as long as they "pretend" to be Lutheran. They need to step forward in honesty. Why won't they do that? I believe it's all about money, folks. They have more than 46,000 alumni—most of whom graduated from a Lutheran college with a Lutheran heritage. To acknowledge who Capital really is today potentially jeopardizes the loyalty and giving of its alumni.

What does this say about spiritual blindness and its hold on America? As alumni drive by Capital's campus, they see a university they know and love. Even though I now personally believe that Capital was never what it could have been because the Bible was taught doctrinally and not in its entirety, it once was a Christian institution based on the beliefs of the Lutheran Church. The "shell" or "showroom" of the university is still intact and proud. It is the "core"— "the warehouse"—that is now spiritually decayed, though its lack of biblical literacy has had it dying for years. The school is promoting and honoring diversity rather than honoring Jesus Christ but is willing to take money from everyone, while diluting its truth in order to preserve its status. Does Jesus honor either diversity or dishonesty? Absolutely not.

Digging a little deeper into Capital's core, when asked about religious education there, the president stated that students are required to take two years of religion. One semester must be Christian religion, and the other three semesters can be religion in any form. Folks, religion taught in "any form"—particularly at a supposed Christian college—is no religion at all. Lutheran parents who send their son or daughter to Capital, a Lutheran university, want them to learn Lutheran doctrine. Though I no longer support Lutheran doctrine, I understand how those parents feel. It is fine to learn about other religions while in college. It is not fine to honor any religion there that is not Biblical and does not accept the teachings of the Triune God. It is my desire that Capital teach the Bible in its entirety. Since that's not possible (at least it hasn't been done for its history), shouldn't they at least teach a lot of the Bible the majority of the time?

Capital University in its present form is a reflective mirror of America. The outer shell of America, like Capital, loudly proclaims and proudly stands up for its religious heritage, just as Europe once did. At its core, however, America, like Capital, is at best weakly connected to its Creator. Capital, I believe, is no longer a Christian university. Instead of knowing and proclaiming the Bible, it long ago caved into the world in the name of diversity—one of Satan's greatest educational tools of divisiveness. Claiming diversity over Christ has made Capital just another school—one of many—that no longer honors God. It has written its own Bible and is spiritually blind, nearing death. It is certainly dead as a Lutheran university.

The same is true of America. President Obama has announced to the world that we are no longer a Christian nation. God is removed as often as possible from every phase of our nation. President Obama didn't even recognize our long-standing National Day of Prayer. Our own people are turning on us, proudly claiming their allegiance to Allah, and making plans to destroy us.

Jesus Himself said, "As in the days of Noah, so shall the coming of the Son of Man be." Jesus predicted the fall of Capital and America a long time ago. No one paid attention because Satan was marvelous in his plan of the deception of mankind. God left us a Bible, just one book, to read—one that carries all truth, including knowledge of when and how mankind will once again fall into the sin of Noah's day—but few have read it. How have you missed it? How has Capital missed it? How has America missed it? It has been missed because people haven't cared enough to read the entire Bible and then have believed anything and anyone they want to believe. Capital missed it because they failed to read the whole Bible and relied on doctrine instead of the Word. Is that true of you, too? It is obviously true of the Capital alumna who, as a pastor's wife, proudly stated that God created homosexuals. Nothing in the Bible supports that—absolutely nothing! Yet, she took a firm, public, anti-biblical stand in March, even to a stranger. Read your Bible, folks. Prove me wrong.

I am personally saddened by the fall of Capital, but I'm even sadder that America's spirituality is either dead or dying. My hope, though, is not in Capital or America. My hope is in Christ and His Word that shows me when, why, and how He came and how He will come again as well as the glory that awaits those who remain true to Him to that end. Let's read our entire Bibles and then all say together, "Amen. Come, Lord Jesus!"

ENDNOTES

[1] Dr. D. James Kennedy, "The Coral Ridge Hour", Nov. 1, 2009, Television Sermon, Coral Ridge Ministries, Ft. Lauderdale, FL.

[2] Dr. Jack Van Impe, "Earth's Golden Age," *Perhaps Today,* July/August 2008, p. 3.

[3] Ken Raggio, "Prophetic Fulfillments in 2005, *Endtime Magazine,* January/February 2006, p. 12.

[4] Ibid., p. 2, 10.

[5] Strobe Talbott, "The Birth of the Global Nation," *Time,* July 20, 1992.

[6] Rob Stein, "FDA Approves Implant That Holds Medical Data," *The Detroit News* (As copied from *The Washington Post)*, October 2007, Health Section.

[7] Liz F. Kay, "ID Chips in Credit Cards, Everyday Items Questioned," *The Detroit News* (As copied from *The Baltimore Sun),* May 2007.

[8] Ed Garsten, "Auto Black Boxes Defended," *The Detroit News,* 2007.

[9] Jack Van Impe, *Perhaps Today,* September-October 2009.

[10] "Lutheran Heritage Foundation Celebrates 15 Years," *The Voice,* November 7, 2007.

[11] Max Lucado, *Fearless,* Illinois: Tyndale House Publishers, 2009, p. 164 & 171.

[12] "Whose Land Is It?," *The Lutheran Witness,* St. Louis: Concordia Publishing House, November 2006, p. 5.

[13] Zola Levitt, *Levitt Letter,* September 2009, p. 5.

[14] "We Are Needed—Are Lutherans Afraid to take on the World?," *The Lutheran Witness,* St. Louis: Concordia Publishing House, November 2006, p. 13.

[15] Ibid.

[16] "More Avoiding Denominational Labels," *Sarasota-Manatee Herald Tribune,* Section A, p. 3, March 9, 2009.

[17] J ohn H. Adams, "PCUSA's Reasons for Staggering Loss of Members Aren't Justified by Numbers," *The Layman Online,* December 1, 2003.

[18] Ibid.

[19] David W. Virtue, "Episcopal Church Fights Declining Ordinations, Clergy Loss, Dwindling Membership," *Virtue Online,* September 30, 2007.

[20] Gerald J. Mendoza, "Why Do Catholics Become Evangelicals," *Homiletic & Pastoral Review,* October 21, 2007.

[21] Ibid.

[22] Dave Welch, "Return Offensive Leadership to the Church," *Levitt Letter,* May 2009, p. 13.

[23] Ethan Bronner, "Israel will Showcase Dead Sea Scrolls over Internet," *The Detroit News* (As copied from the New York Times), August 28, 2008, p. 12A.

[24] Gregg Krupa, "Interfaith Book Shatters Barriers, Fosters Dialogue," *The Detroit News,* November 12, 2007. p. 2B.

[25] Pastor Daniel Johnson, "Too Busy Doing Church," *The Covenant Companion,* October 2009, p. 4.

[26] John E. Phelan Jr., "Why We Worship," *The Covenant Companion,* October 2009, p. 5.

9 781609 572938